September 2015.

For Petra,

This is a little something to thank you for
helping me with IT GIRL. You have no idea
how honoured I am to be working with someone
as talented and skilled as you.
It makes me so happy having you in my life.
Thankyou for being a great friend.

xx

From Doctor

3x3Annual11

THREE BY THREE ILLUSTRATION ANNUAL
SPONSORED BY 3X3 THE MAGAZINE OF CONTEMPORARY ILLUSTRATION

ILLUSTRATION BY SARA CUNHA

CONTENTS

Anna & Elena Balbusso

PICTURE BOOK SHOW JUDGE

The Balbusso twins live and work in Milan. Since 1998 they have been working as a team on projects in Europe, Asia and North America. Their projects include book covers, editorial, in house corporate, advertising, children's books and classic novels. Their artwork has been exhibited in numerous exhibitions and galleries in Italy and abroad. In 2013 they were winners of a V&A Illustration Award and have received recognition from the Society of Illustrators, *3x3 International Illustration Annual*, *Communication Arts*, *American Illustration*, *Spectrum*, *Creative Quarterly*, *Applied Arts* and *Lürzers Archive 200 Best Illustrators*.

Élisabeth Cohat

PICTURE BOOK SHOW JUDGE

After studying graphic design and semiology in Paris at the École des Hautes Études en Sciences Sociales, Élisabeth began her career in the childrens' division at Editions Gallimard—the same year the Folio Junior and "Voiles" departments were created. She was in charge of developing numerous collections such as *Mes premieres Decouvertes* (My First Discoveries) and *Decouverte Gallimard* (Discovery Gallimard), and took part in the creation of innovative concepts across several departments. She was promoted to graphic designer of Guides Gallimard upon its creation in 1990 and assumed her current title of art director for Gallimard Jeunesse in 1999.

Sylvie Frank

PICTURE BOOK SHOW JUDGE

Sylvie is an associate editor at Paula Wiseman Books, an imprint of Simon & Schuster Children's Publishing Division. She edits picture books, middle-grade and YA fiction, and occasionally nonfiction. Recent books she has edited include *Storm* by Donna Jo Napoli, *Breathe* by Scott Magoon and *Whistle in the Dark* by Susan Hill Long. One of her favorite pastimes is browsing agents' and illustrators' websites for new talent.

Paul Gonzales

PROFESSIONAL SHOW JUDGE

Paul is a deputy design director for the features department at the *Los Angeles Times*. As such, he leads a team of designers in producing the newspaper's lively and creative Sunday Calendar, Arts & Books and Travel sections. In his 20-plus-year career at the *Times*, he has won many awards for design, art direction and photo illustration from such prestigious organizations as *Communication Arts*, *Print*, The Society for News Design and Society of Publication Designers. His collaboration with illustrators has also resulted in a number of award-winning pieces.

Marieke Griffioen

PROFESSIONAL SHOW JUDGE

Marieke is design director at the Amsterdam office of Edenspiekermann, a design agency with offices in Berlin and San Francisco. She engages illustrators for corporate identities, campaigns, annual reports, brochures and magazines for companies like the Utrecht City Theater, MN pension management, Eindhoven Technical University, Robeco Sam and Twijnstra Gudde

Jim Hoover

PICTURE BOOK SHOW JUDGE

Jim is an Associate Art Director at Viking Children's Books in New York. A graduate of the Rhode Island School of Design in Illustration, Jim has been in publishing now for over twelve years. He has designed and art directed well over one-hundred titles including *John Lennon: All I Want Is The Truth*, *Stuck In The Middle*, *Marching For Freedom*, *Titanic SinKS!*, *Mission Control: This Is Apollo* and the children's book adaptation of Al Gore's *An Inconvenient Truth*.

Tim J Luddy

PROFESSIONAL SHOW JUDGE

Tim has worked as a designer and art director in New York and San Francisco, for publications including *Mother Jones*, *BusinessWeek*, *eCompany Now!* (also known as *Business 2.0*,) *PC World*, and *Diablo*. He has lectured on publication design at UC Berkeley, the California College of Art, San Francisco State University, and the University of San Francisco. *Mother Jones* received the National Magazine Award for General Excellence twice during his tenure there. His work has been recognized by the Society of Publication Designers and *Print* magazine. He also teaches yoga in San Francisco.

Robert Meganck

STUDENT SHOW JUDGE

Robert is a professor of illustration, graphic design and digital imaging and Chair of the Department of Communication Arts at Virginia Commonwealth University. He is currently in his 35th year at VCU. He is a freelance illustrator and president of Communication Design. Robert has received over 300 regional, national and international awards for his research and professional practice in illustration and graphic design. His current research includes the development of an interactive dimensional model of color space, a project that is being co-authored by Matt Wallin, *Communication Arts* and Peter Martin.

Robert Neubecker

Doug Panton

Andy Potts

Mark Smith

Durwin Talon

Jamie Trendall

Klaas Verplancke

PICTURE BOOK SHOW JUDGE

Robert draws for the *New York Times*, the *Chicago Tribune*, Slate.com and *The Wall Street Journal*. His first book for children, *Wow! City!* won an American Library Association Notable book award. More than twenty books have followed including: *Every Corner Needs a Monster* with Jean Reidy, *I Got Two Dogs* with John Lithgow, and *Sophie Peterman Tells the Truth* with Sarah Weeks. *What Little Boys Are Made Of* won the 2012 Kirkus Review Best Books of the Year award. His most recent books include *Linus the Vegetarian T-Rex* and *Winter is for Snow*. Robert has taught at School of Visual Arts in New York, BYU and the University of Utah.

STUDENT SHOW JUDGE

Doug is an Illustrator and educator based in Toronto. Chair of the First Program area for the past five years he is also teaches in the Illustration faculty at OCAD University. Over the years he has worked with clients from all around the world and his illustrations have received recognition from publications such as *3×3, Creative Quarterly, American Illustration* SILA and *Applied Arts*. His clients include the *New York Times, Wall Street Journal, The Walrus Magazine, Reader's Digest*, and Oxford University Press.

STUDENT SHOW JUDGE

Andy is a London-based illustrator and animator, originally from Kingswinford in the UK. He graduated with a BA Hons degree in illustration from Portsmouth University and his career has encompassed image making, animation, graphic design and art direction including seven years as Lead Designer at Abbey Road Studios. Since going freelance he has been commissioned by a variety of clients in advertising, publishing and design. His eye-catching images have appeared in many international newspapers and magazines.

PROFESSIONAL SHOW JUDGE

Working out of Exeter in the Southwest of England, Mark's illustrations have been featured in newspapers, magazines, books and in advertising campaigns around the world. His work has also won international recognition from the likes of the NY Society of Illustrators, LA Society of Illustrators, *American Illustration, 3x3 Magazine*, the V&A Illustration awards, *Communication Arts*, the Society of Publication Designers and more.

STUDENT SHOW JUDGE

Durwin is an illustrator, comic book creator, designer and educator. He has produced work for DC Comics, Oni Press, Image Comics, Archaia/ Boom! and White Wolf Publishing. He has also written for TwoMorrows Publishing and Dark Horse Comics. He currently teaches Illustration at Emily Carr University of Art + Design in Vancouver. *Beautiful Scars*, a graphic novel created in collaboration with Guin Thompson was released in March 2014 by Archaia/ Boom! Comics and Simon & Schuster.

STUDENT SHOW JUDGE

Jamie is a magazine art director based in London. He has over 15 years experience working for companies such as the BBC, the *Times*, Haymarket Publishing, as well as design studios. Commissioning illustrators has played a key of part in his work and he has been privileged to have been a judge for the Association of Illustrators and Transport for London's Art on the Underground.

PROFESSIONAL SHOW JUDGE

Klaas is a full-time illustrator in Bruges. At first glance, his drawings and paintings differ a great deal in appearance and execution. But they always display the qualities that characterize him as an illustrator and designer: a sense of humor that can vary from mild to sardonic, a poetic imagination, a preference for illustrating abstract concepts and universal emotions–and a side ways, surrealistic view of reality. He has been honored with a whole series of national and international awards, nominations and selections, culminating in winning the Bologna Ragazzi Award, a bronze medal in the *3x3 Picture Book Show* and a selection for the *Original Art Show* by the Society of Illustrators.

WELCOME TO THE ELEVENTH ANNUAL COMPILATION OF WHAT HAS BECOME ONE OF THE FEW, IF ONLY, ILLUSTRATION ANNUALS WITH A DISTINCT INTERNATIONAL FLAVOR. AND ONE WITH A LOT OF FRESH FACES THIS YEAR. AS YOU MAY IMAGINE THERE ARE DIFFERENCES AMONG ILLUSTRATION ANNUALS. THERE ARE THOSE JUDGED PRIMARILY BY ILLUSTRATORS. THOSE THAT ARE ASSOCIATED WITH ORGANIZATIONS. OR THOSE WHICH ARE NOT SOLELY ILLUSTRA-TION-FOCUSSED. BUT THERE IS ONLY ONE INDEPENDENT INTERNATIONAL ANNUAL WHOSE MISSION IS TO PRESERVE, PROTECT AND PROMOTE ILLUSTRATION ACROSS ALL BORDERS. YOU'RE HOLDING IT IN YOUR HANDS. THIS YEAR OUR PANEL OF JUDGES—A SELECT GROUP OF INTERNATIONAL ART DIRECTORS AND DESIGNERS WHO COMMISSION ILLUSTRATION FOR NEWSPAPERS, MAGAZINES, BOOKS, CHILDREN'S BOOKS, ADVERTISING AND A WIDE VARIETY OF ASSIGNMENTS—JOINED BY A EQUALLY DISTINGUISHED GROUP OF ILLUSTRATORS VIEWED NEARLY 5,000 IMAGES TO SELECT THE 392 WINNERS. AND THIS YEAR WE ADDED AN HONOR-ABLE MENTION CATEGORY WITH 537 ADDITIONAL WINNERS WHO ARE SHOWCASED ONLINE. OUR JUDGES WORKED INDEPENDENTLY OVER A TWO-WEEK PERIOD WITHOUT CONSULTATION. THEY HAD NO QUOTA, NO MAGIC NUMBER THEY TRIED TO REACH. THEY WERE ONLY CHARGED WITH SELECTING THE VERY BEST. DO WE HAVE EVERY ILLUSTRATOR REPRESENTED? NO, BUT WE DO HAVE AN EXPANSIVE SELECTION OF WORK FROM ALL PARTS OF THE WORLD THAT HAS MET THE STANDARD OF EXCELLENCE WE STRIVE FOR HERE AT 3X3. *ENJOY!*

—THE PUBLISHER

CHRIS BUZELLI *is totally committed to furthering the future of illustration, gaining fairness in fees and protecting an artist's work. Sitting with Chris you'll hear familiar refrains about the trials and tribulations of working in today's contentious legal landscape. Where time must be spent justifying not only the fee but the usage before a job can even begin. If you ask how's teaching going, you'll see a glimmer in his eye as he talks about the latest student who is well on their way to becoming an illustrator. While he doesn't take full-credit for their success you do hear how loudly his former student's laud his personal approach to teaching. Juggling commissions and teaching can be tricky especially when you're as busy as Chris is. Teaching at his alma mater includes a weekly seven-hour bus ride to Providence plus another five hours in the classroom. Grueling, yet he'll tell you it's not tiring, it's inspiring to be with the students. With his continued dedication to the field of illustration and his commitment to guiding the next generation of illustrators we are pleased to honor him as our 3x3 Illustrator/Educator of the Year, 2014.*

Q Tell us about your early schooling, did you always want to be an artist?

A Honestly I never thought that I could choose "artist" as a profession until my senior year in high school, it just wasn't a realistic option in the south suburbs of Chicago. My mother is a nurse and my father was a machinist who worked in various steel/glass factories in the city. While my family wasn't artistic but I think they saw that I had an interest in the arts and have always fully supported me in every way.

Q What were some of your early influences?

A Definitely my grandfather. I spent weekends with my grandparents who ran a local television repair shop from their home. There was this painting show we'd watch on PBS with Bill Alexander and when I was seven or eight years old my grandfather bought his "Magic Paintbrush Set." He'd set up the two easels in his shop and we'd paint together almost every weekend. I look back now and think I also learned a lot about how to run a business from my grandparents.

There was also a wonderful art teacher in high school whom I consider a great friend today. He introduced me to the art of Paul Cadmus and his *Seven Deadly Sins*, it was the first time that a piece of art grabbed me in a real way. The series of paintings done in the 40s were filled with smart and beautiful concepts that coincided with each sin. They sparked a desire in me to do the same— to conceptually and visually

communicate with paint. I didn't really know it at the time, but this experience set me on my path towards illustration.

Q How did you get your first big break?

A I really never had a first big break, my career began as a very slow burn. After I graduated from Rhode Island of School of Design (RISD) I moved to New York City and quickly realized that illustration wasn't going to pay the rent. I was getting illustration work but nothing steady so I had several part-time jobs. But I was still putting in a full day of illustration work at my studio—a small desk in the corner of my shared living room—usually creating projects for myself or working on promos and business stuff. It took about seven years until I felt I could call myself a full-time illustrator.

Q Your work is mostly editorial, have you had any opportunity to work in advertising?

A I think for the past few years I've have worked on more advertising assignments than previously. Working in advertising is a much different beast than editorial. The pay of course is much greater but so is the usage. Advertising also entails a bit more work due to all the cooks in the kitchen—ad agency art directors, the client and sometimes the lawyers. The trick is to come away with an image that satisfies not only the client but also yourself.

Q How is today's work different than when you were first starting out?

A In the beginning I'd incorporate a lot of collage into my illustrations. And I was doing what I thought illustration was—lots of businessmen with telescopes and briefcases on rocket ships— you get the idea. And I was overly influenced by my favorite illustrators at the time.

But about twelve years ago I made

an abrupt and huge shift in the way I approach illustration. I tore my ACL in a basketball game and got stuck up in my fifth floor walk-up for several months. That isolation gave me time to think and really focus on my career instead of worrying about each illustration job. I went back to drawing and painting the things that interested me creating five paintings using visual language from my own experiences and my personal work. Those images became the foundation of my current work. I've never looked back.

Q Talk with us a bit about your process?

A It starts with the sketches. I usually do about 20 to 30 quick thumbnails for each project—banging my head on my drawing board a few times in between. Then go back over them and revise the ones that have potential. Then hopefully I'll have about three ideas that could work for the assignment and ones that I'm personally happy with. I've been lucky to have strong relationships with a few art directors that allow for some experimentation, change and growth within my illustration projects.

Q What do you think about the current state of illustration?

A I started in an industry that seemed to put an emphasis on sticking to one style and not being able to dabble in other avenues of illustration. The industry even seemed to draw a distinction between different types of editorial illustrators. Happily, those restrictions are starting to disappear; it's not uncommon to see editorial illustrators working on children's books or illustrating graphic novel covers. Editorial illustrators can work on ad campaigns, work in an animation studio, create a zine, sell work in galleries. Or even design their own clothing line.

Sadly the financial part, the fees for illustration have not changed since I started. It's a constant struggle for many of us to push for fair budgets these days. And when I started contracts were simply an email with "first rights only." Today they've become lengthy and confusing pages of over-reaching rights for usage. I have to spend an hour or more amending the contract, negotiating with the art director, or the person in charge of contracts, before I can even start the job.

Q Do you approach your personal work differently than your commercial work?

A My commercial work is my personal work. I try and make sure that the content and imagery of my commissions are worthy of hanging on a wall. It's not possible 100% of the time but that's the goal.

Q Have you ever had an artist representative?

A A few years after I graduated I joined a very large illustration rep firm. I thought they were going to be the magic key that I needed in order to "make it" as an illustrator. I made a crucial mistake in thinking that I could just concentrate on painting and they would take care of everything else. And while I did get some bigger illustration assignments than on my own I had to give back a large chunk of money to the rep for the work they got me—and for the work that was coming directly to me. During those years I neglected the business side of my career and  missed many opportunities. However, I'm not totally anti-rep, I actually have a rep now. The firm is much smaller and concentrates on getting work other than editorial.

Q Let's talk about your experiences as a teacher, you've been teaching since 1998 right?

A Actually I started teaching even earlier. I was teaching art classes to inner-city kids and kids with learning disabilities during my RISD years Those young students were the toughest students that I have ever had to teach, but it was great training for me.

When one of my professors at RISD started teaching at the University of Hartford I was offered a teaching position there. And after a couple of years Jordin Isip asked if I'd like to take over his editorial illustration class at RISD.

Those first few years at Hartford and RISD were very bumpy and frustrating for me as a teacher. It was a learn-on-the-job situation, I was trying to my best but I think I came off as a blustery young punk. Luckily there were some great professors to riff off of since I had very little practical illustration experience. Now with many more years of experience in the illustration field I'm much more confident teaching. I really enjoy the teaching process and constantly change assignments to keep it exciting for both me and the students.

Q How are you able to juggle teaching and commissions?

A I teach up at RISD once a week, it's a seven-hour round bus trip and the class is five hours. Those seven hours every Thursday have become my office hours, so if you email me I'll usually get back to you Thursday (unless it's a client). I actually look forward to those once a week trips, I have time to read a book, watch a movie or just think. The trip is a good break in my illustration work week.

I can't say that teaching never interrupts my commissioned work but I try hard to not let it get in the way. Sometimes I work late nights and weekends to make up for the day out of the studio. But I think teaching actually gives back more than it takes away.

I've learned much as a teacher by having to verbally communicate my thoughts about concepts and the practical methods of illustration. My students are a constant source of inspiration.

Q Do you think there's a secret to why so many successful young illustrators came out of the program you are teaching?

A The big secret is hard work and curiosity. I'm fortunate to get students in their senior year, they've had incredible teachers along the way that have readied them with strong academic drawing and thinking skills. I'm a small cog in the giant machine of their academic career. I'm teaching them the practice of illustration and letting them know what's in store for them. I put them through a sort of illustration boot

camp and don't hold back. I try to be as honest and forthcoming as possible during our crits. I try to pull out the unique passion in every student and build upon it without too much hand-holding. I give them as many real-world assignments in order to teach the nuances that are missed during class assignments. I truly want them to succeed and give them every tool possible. I've also had some really hard-working, passionate and curious students in my career, it gives me great satisfaction to see that many are having success in this very difficult profession.

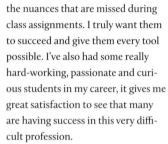

Q Do you feel there is anything missing in today's education of an illustrator?

A There is always something missing, there's always more. I wish my seniors had a business class taught by a business professional and a class in contract negotiations taught by a legal expert. I wish they had a class in proper email communication and networking. I touch on these topics during my class, but I think the students all need more in order to really prepare them for the real world.

Q What are your responsibilities as an instructor?

A Simply give my students the tools in order to have a chance to make it in the illustration world. Show them that their mistakes are sometimes surprisingly their personal voice. Give them honest and constructive crits. Push them to their limits.

Q Your advice to graduates entering the field today?

A Immerse yourself in the illustration field and community if you really want to make it your life's work. Think about the long game when making business decisions. It's easy to get hired for a few illustration jobs after graduating but it's very difficult to make illustration your life's career.

Q And finally, what's in your future?

A I can hardly wait for the next project and hope I can keep doing what I'm doing until I'm too old to hold a pencil. I enjoy the balance of teaching once a week and hope to continue that for just as long.

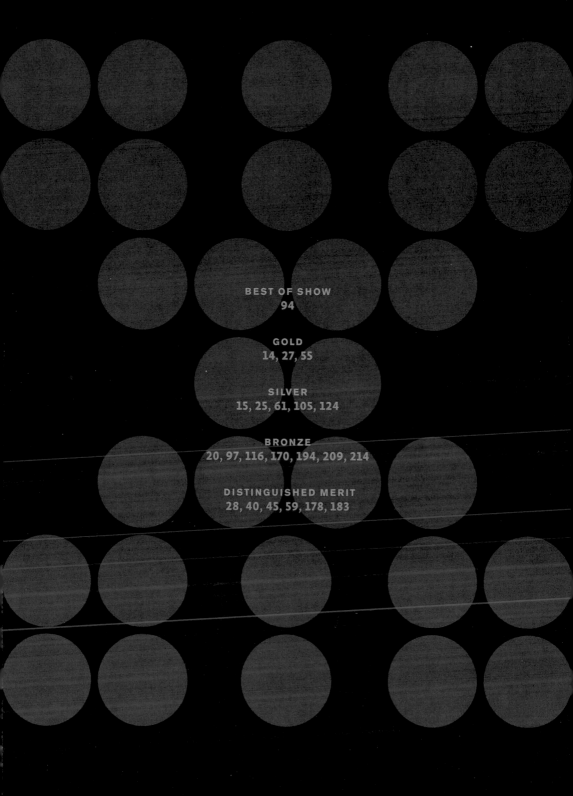

BEST OF SHOW
94

GOLD
14, 27, 55

SILVER
15, 25, 61, 105, 124

BRONZE
20, 97, 116, 170, 194, 209, 214

DISTINGUISHED MERIT
28, 40, 45, 59, 178, 183

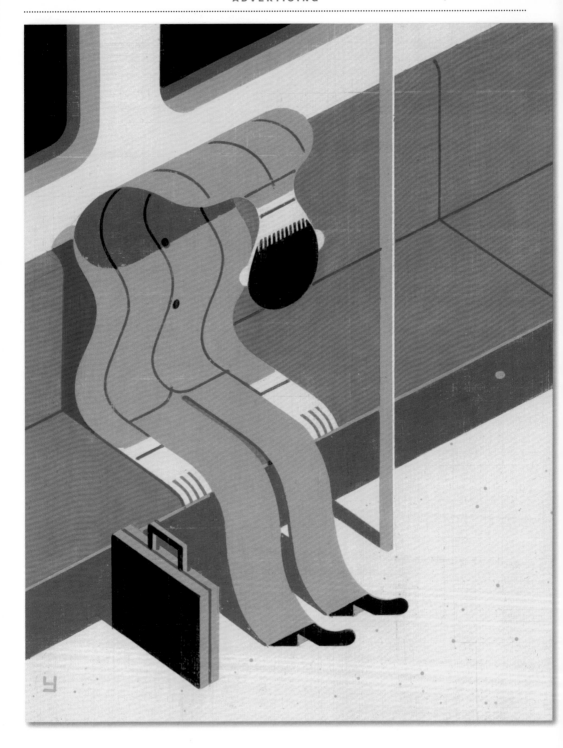

GOLD *Brad Yeo*

SILVER *Bill Mayer*

THE ARTWORKS

share the holiday spirit

No. 5

klippan wool blankets, indian cashmere scarf, texcelus stuffed toy

No. 3

assorted glassware

No. 8

smith corona typewriter, life japanese paper, assorted writing instruments

(L) *Studio Tipi* (R) *Carlos Araujo*

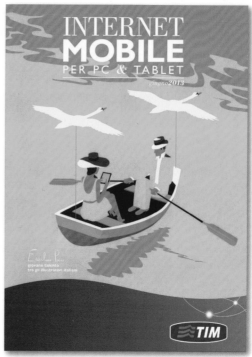

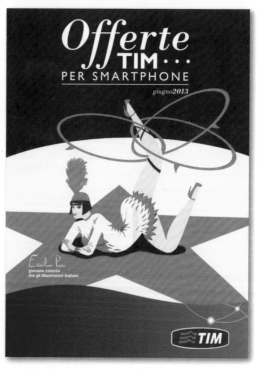

Emiliano Ponzi

Otto Steininger

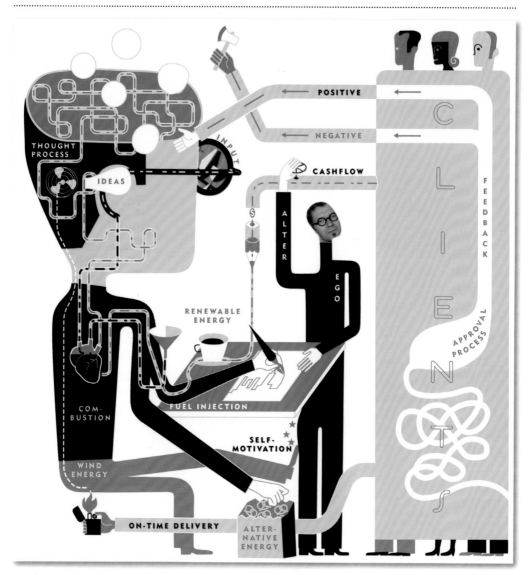

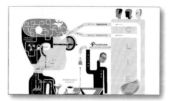

Otto Steininger

André da Loba

(L) *Andy Potts* (R) SILVER *Anna and Elena Balbusso*

DISTINGUISHED MERIT *Anna and Elena Balbusso*

Michael Glenwood

Rick Sealock

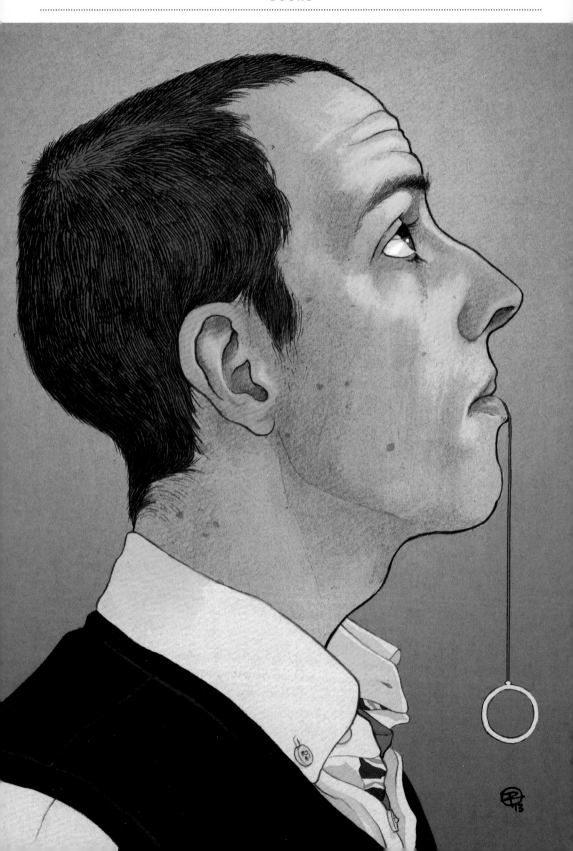

Bill Mayer

Bill Mayer

Matt Duffin

DISTINGUISHED MERIT *Curt Merlo*

Pierre Pratt

THE CRITICS

FICTION

CHARACTER STUDIES

THE WAR

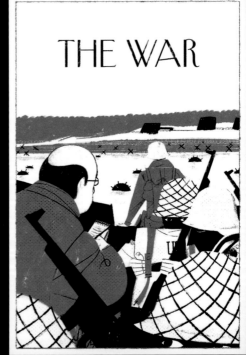

(L) *Simone Massoni* (R) *Cun Shi*

(L) *Golden Cosmos* (R) DISTINGUISHED MERIT *Bill Mayer*

蟾蜍

CH'AN CHU: THE LUCKY MONEY TOAD

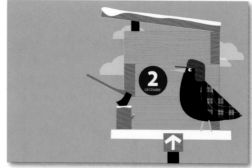

(L) *Bill Mayer* (R) *Julien Chung*

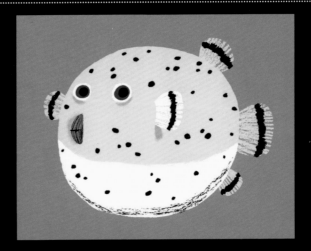

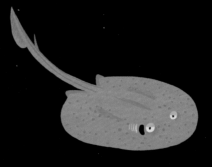

André Letria

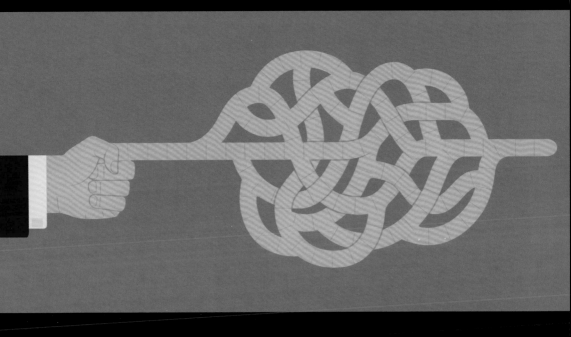

Aad Goudappel

Aad Goudappel

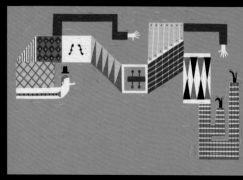

Catarina Sobral

MARTINO GOZZI
Giovani promesse

UNIVERSALE
ECONOMICA
FELTRINELLI

(L) *Emiliano Ponzi* (R) *Aad Goudappel*

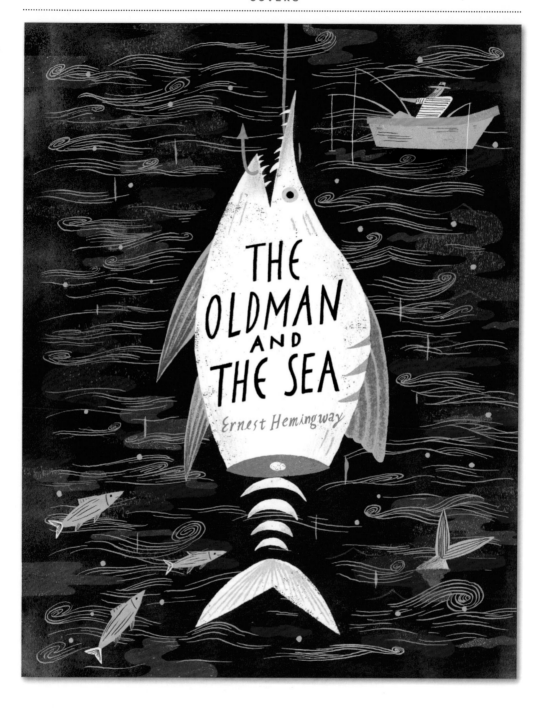

THE OLDMAN AND THE SEA

Ernest Hemingway

(L) *Yeji Yun* (R) GOLD *Valeria Petrone*

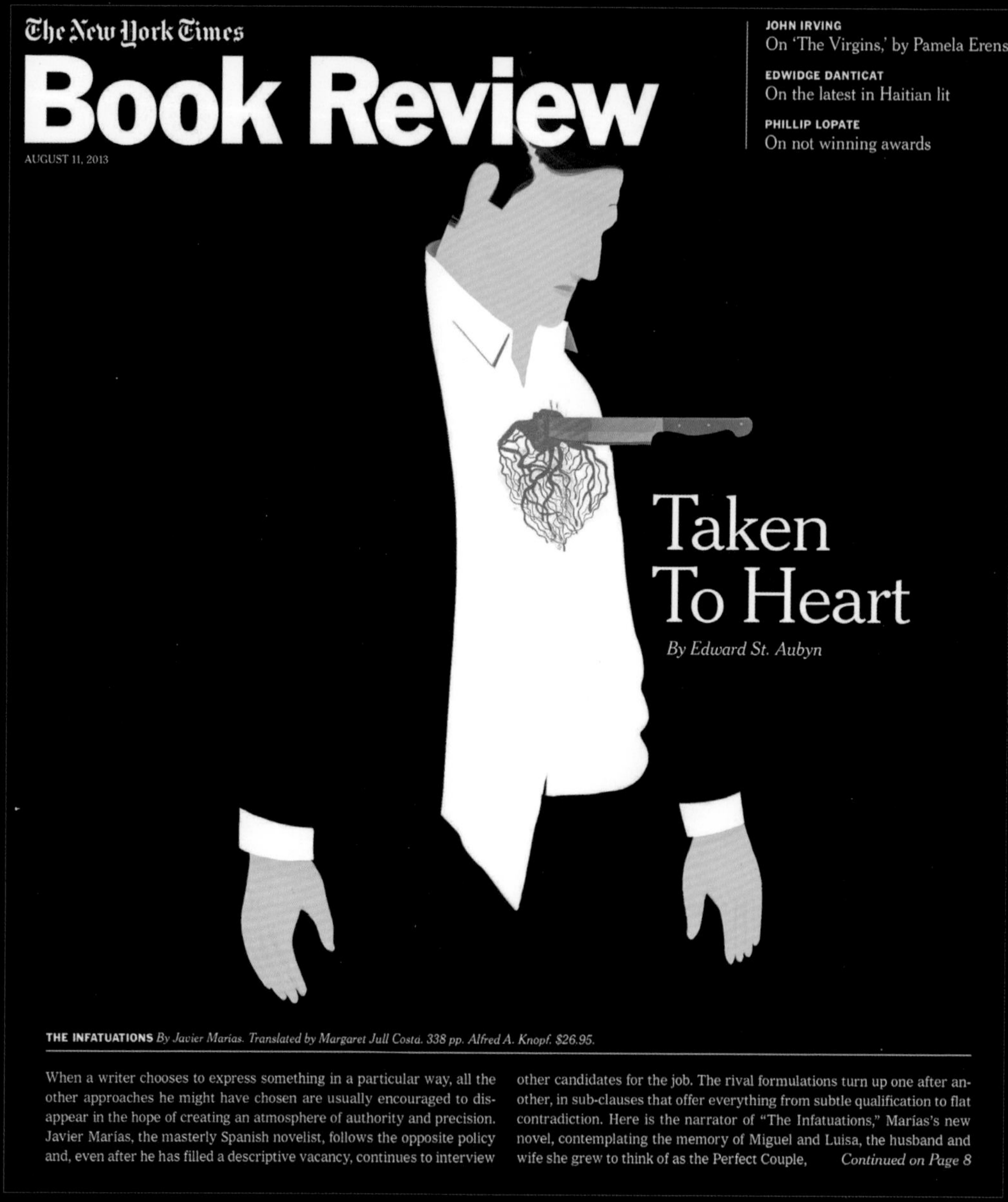

The New York Times

Book Review

AUGUST 11, 2013

JOHN IRVING
On 'The Virgins,' by Pamela Erens

EDWIDGE DANTICAT
On the latest in Haitian lit

PHILLIP LOPATE
On not winning awards

Taken To Heart

By Edward St. Aubyn

THE INFATUATIONS *By Javier Marías. Translated by Margaret Jull Costa. 338 pp. Alfred A. Knopf. $26.95.*

When a writer chooses to express something in a particular way, all the other approaches he might have chosen are usually encouraged to disappear in the hope of creating an atmosphere of authority and precision. Javier Marías, the masterly Spanish novelist, follows the opposite policy and, even after he has filled a descriptive vacancy, continues to interview other candidates for the job. The rival formulations turn up one after another, in sub-clauses that offer everything from subtle qualification to flat contradiction. Here is the narrator of "The Infatuations," Marías's new novel, contemplating the memory of Miguel and Luisa, the husband and wife she grew to think of as the Perfect Couple, *Continued on Page 8*

Emiliano Ponzi

John Parra

Week THE ender

N° 10

MAGAZIN FÜR EINBLICKE UND AUSFLÜGE

EUR 8,– (D) CHF 12,– / EUR 10,– (EU)

BELGIEN * NIEDERLANDE
REITWEIN * KUBA * BELGRAD
SÜDAFRIKA * NEW YORK
SPANIEN * TESSIN

DISTINGUISHED MERIT *Brad Holland*

Istvan Banyai

SILVER *Matt Duffin*

(L) *Ben Jones* (R) *Alex Nabaum*

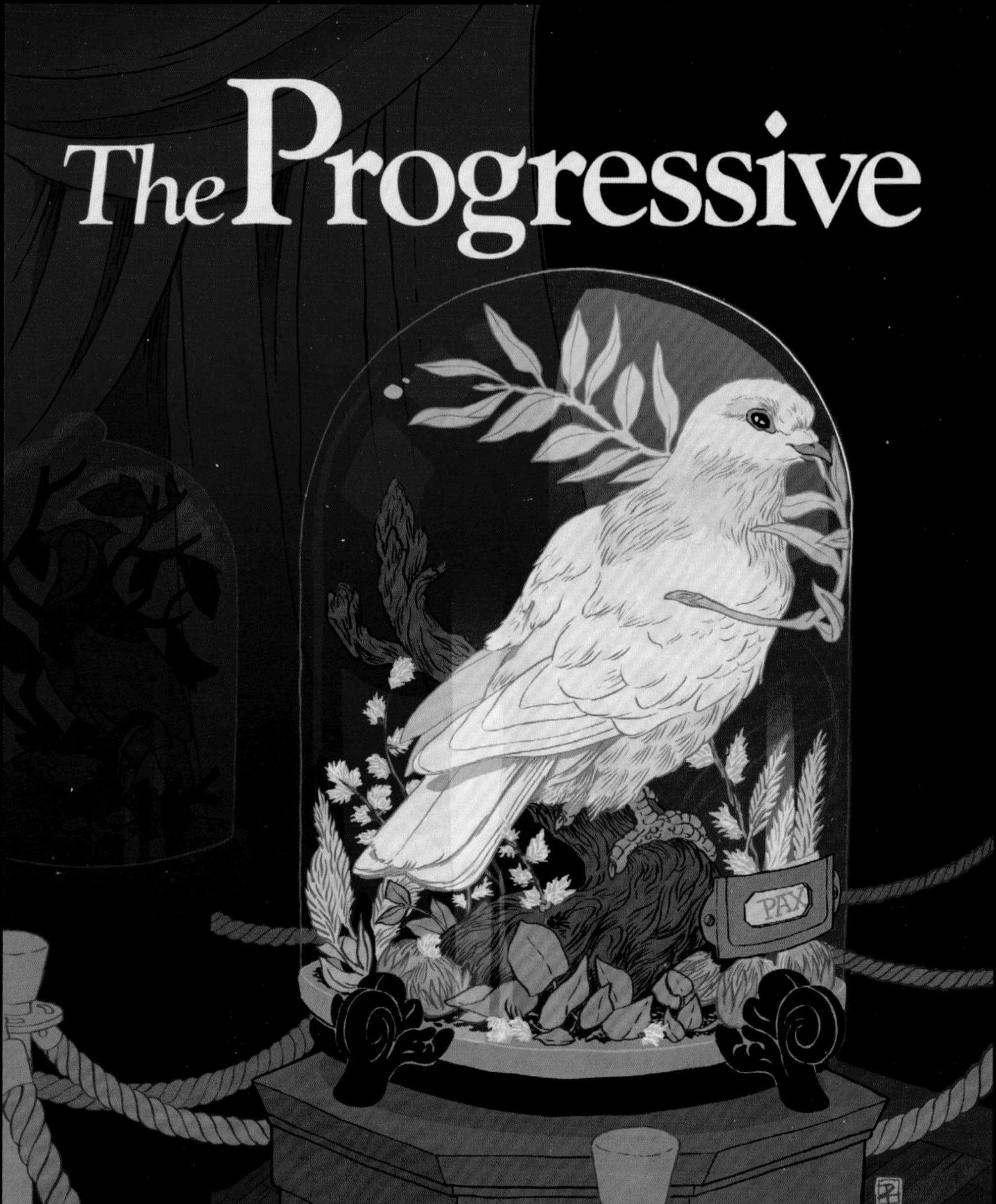
The Progressive
PAX

Peter Diamond

Polly Becker

André Carrilho

Omer Hoffmann

Emiliano Ponzi

Emiliano Ponzi

Anna and Elena Balbusso

(L) *Mügluck* (R) *Klaas Verplancke*

Emiliano Ponzi

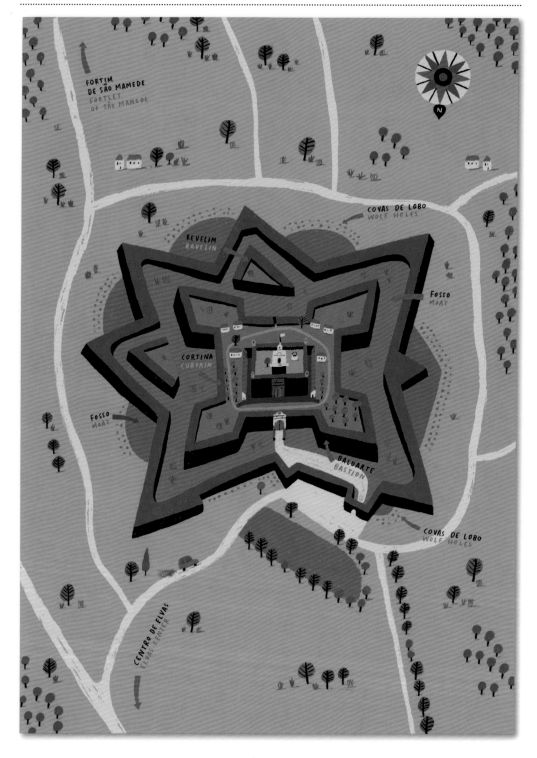

André Letria

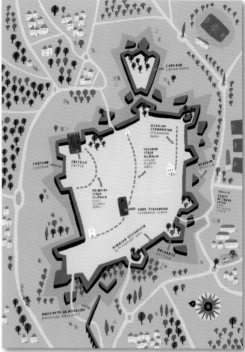

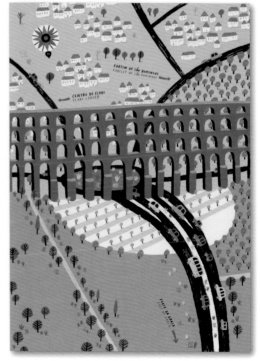

(L) *Jordin Isip* (T) *Andrew Zbihlyj* (B) *Zara Picken*

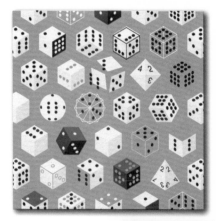

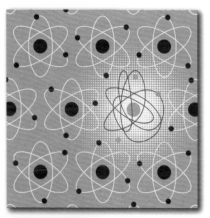

(L) *Daniel Zender* (R) *Keith Negley*

Bill Mayer

(L) *Bill Mayer* (R) *Valeria Petrone*

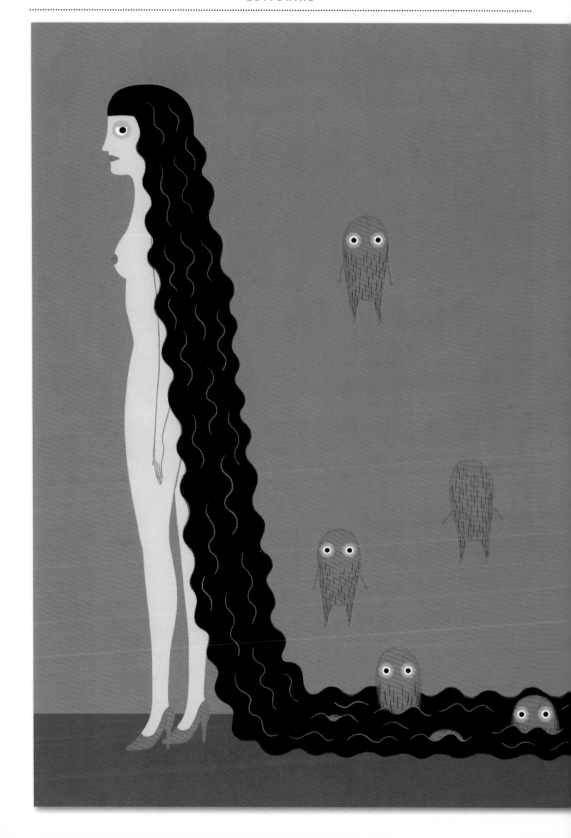

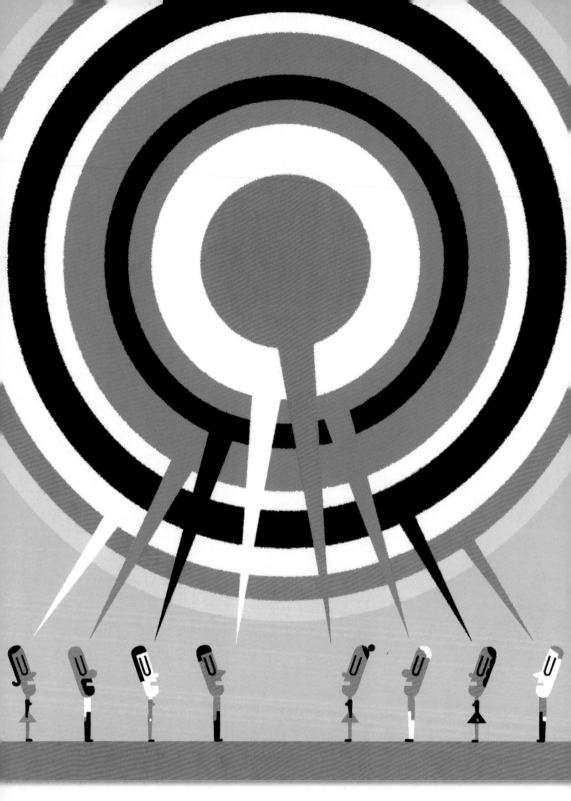

Luc Melanson

Francesco Bongiorni

Magoz

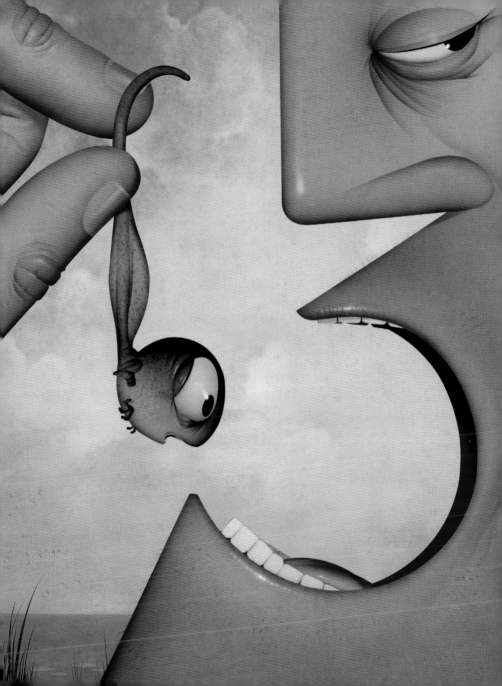

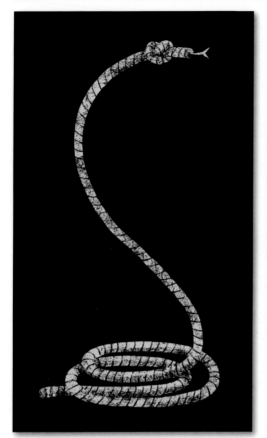

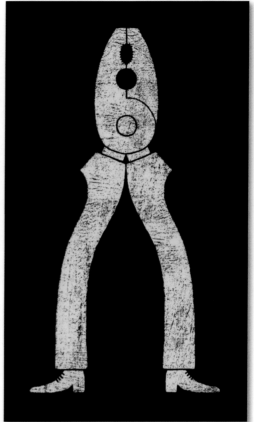

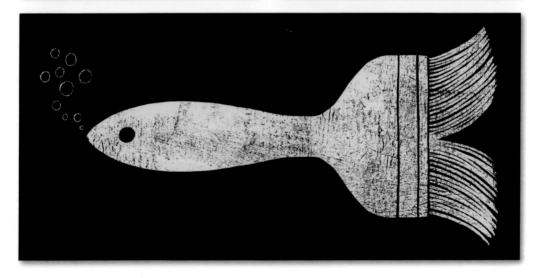

André Letria

Jon Krause

James Steinberg

(L) **BEST OF SHOW** *Mark Smith* (T) *Shaw Nielsen* (B) *Jon Krause*

Sébastien Thibault

BRONZE *Emiliano Ponzi*

(L) *Francesco Bongiorni* (R) *Edel Rodriguez*

Mirko Cresta

Edel Rodriguez

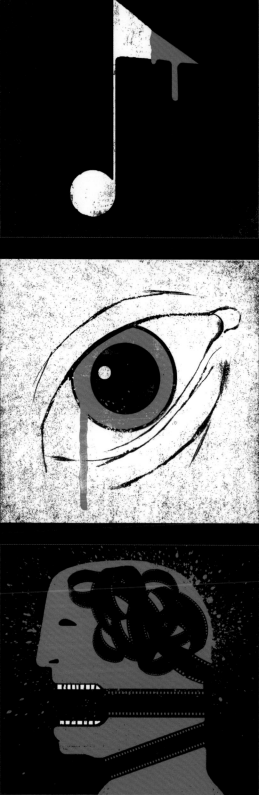

SILVER *Nigel Buchanan*

Peter Donnelly

Paul Wearing

Paul Wearing

André Carrilho

Nigel Buchanan

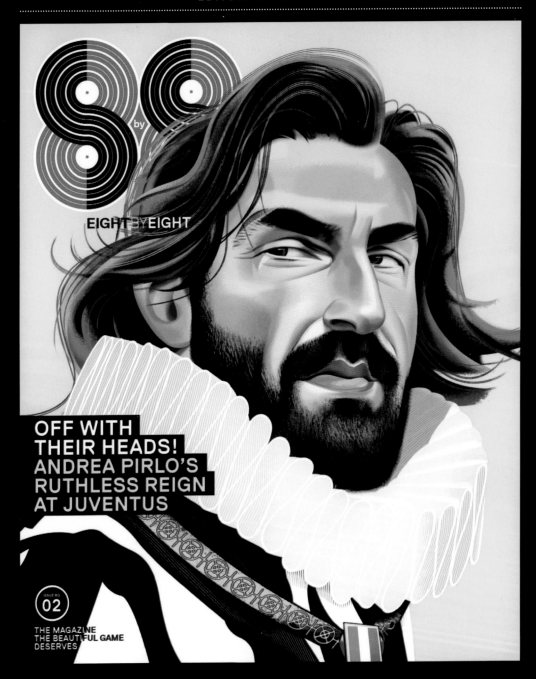

EIGHT BY EIGHT

OFF WITH THEIR HEADS! ANDREA PIRLO'S RUTHLESS REIGN AT JUVENTUS

ISSUE NO.
02

THE MAGAZINE
THE BEAUTIFUL GAME
DESERVES

Nigel Buchanan

Mike Benny

Andrew Zbihlyj

(L) BRONZE *Mark Smith* (R) *Mark Smith*

(L) *Gracia Lam* (R) *Karen Greenberg*

(L) *Francesco Bongiorni* (R) *Emiliano Ponzi*

The Siamese
Amelia & Cordelia

Kira Shaimanova

Hugh D'Andrade

SILVER *Olaf Hajek*

Alice Wellinger

Sylvie Daigneault

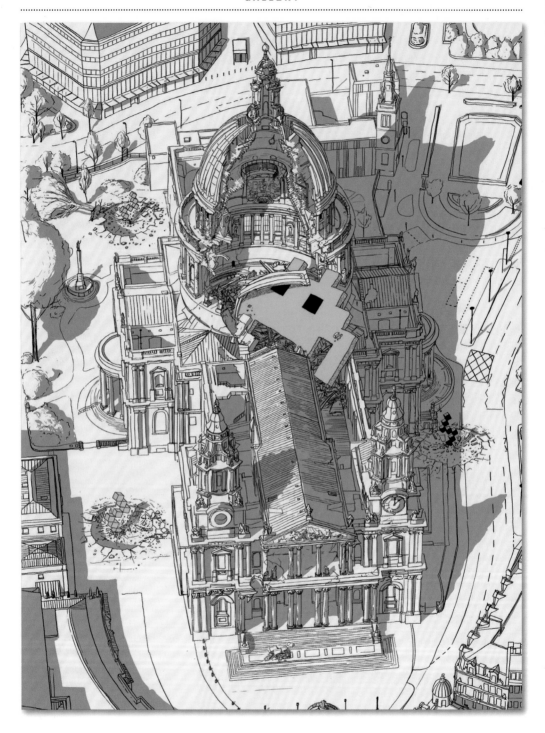

Raid71

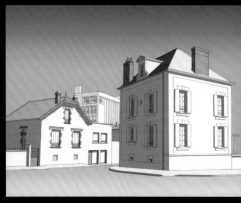

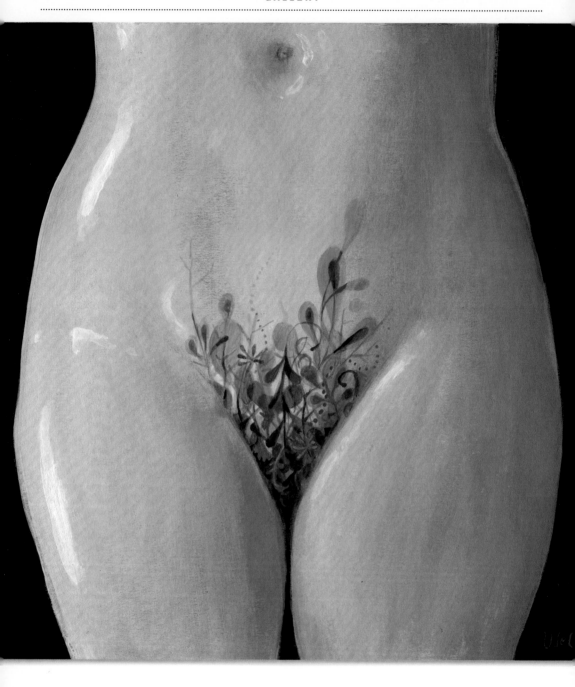

(L) *Alice Wellinger* (R) *Guy Billout*

Michael John Nolan

Page Tsou

Pol Turgeon

Anita Kunz

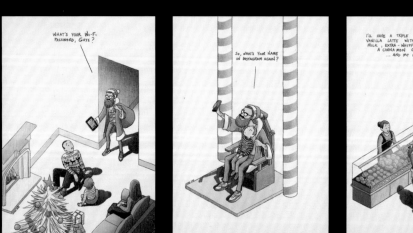

Otto Steininger

Michael Zavacky

Mark McGinnis

Studio Tipi

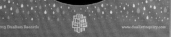

BLOOMERY
SweetShine

BLOOMERY
SweetShine

BLOOMERY
SweetShine

BLOOMERY
SweetShine

BLOOMERY
SweetShine

COCOA

Melinda Beck

JULIEN CHUNG RITZENHOFF

BAYERISCHE STAATSOPER

C—A—M—P—U—S
9./10./11. Dezember 2011

ANDY PAPE

Sigurd der Drachentöter

Kinderoper ab 9 Jahren

Musikalische Leitung
**CHRISTOPHER
WARD**

Inszenierung
**SAM
BROWN**

Bühne und Kostüm
**ANNEMARIE
WOODS**

Licht
**MICHAEL
BAUER**

**Probengebäude am
Marstallplatz**

LOYALTY PARTNER   INFORMATION/KARTEN   089.21851920   WWW.STAATSOPER.DE

BAYERISCHE STAATSOPER

CAMPUS

KARLHEINZ STOCKHAUSEN

Der kleine Harlekin

Musiktheater
für Kinder ab 5 Jahren und Erwachsene

25. / 28. / 30. MÄRZ 2014
2. / 4. / 6. APRIL 2014

Inszenierung
**CARLUS PADRISSA
& FURA DELS BAUS**

Bühne
ROLAND OLBETER

Video
FRANC ALEU

Kostüme
CHU UROM

Licht
REINHARD TRAUB

Probengebäude am Marstallplatz

INFORMATION/KARTEN   WWW.STAATSOPER.DE

BAYERISCHE STAATSOPER

C—A—M—P—U—S
17./18./19./12.2010

KINDEROPER NACH „THE FAIRY QUEEN"
VON HENRY PURCELL

Nepomuks Nacht

Musikalische Leitung
**STELLARIO
FAGONE**

Inszenierung
**ANDREAS
LUTZENBERGER**

Bühne
**ANDREA
HAJEK**

Kostüme
**CLAUDIA
HALL**

Licht
**THERESA
MAYR**

Bearbeitung
**URSULA
GESSAT**

**PROBENGEBÄUDE AM
MARSTALLPLATZ**

INFORMATION/KARTEN   WWW.STAATSOPER.DE

László Nagy

MOUTON NOIR

F I F T Y   M E N

APRIL 19 * THE BLACK SHEEP INN

Edel Rodriguez

László Nagy

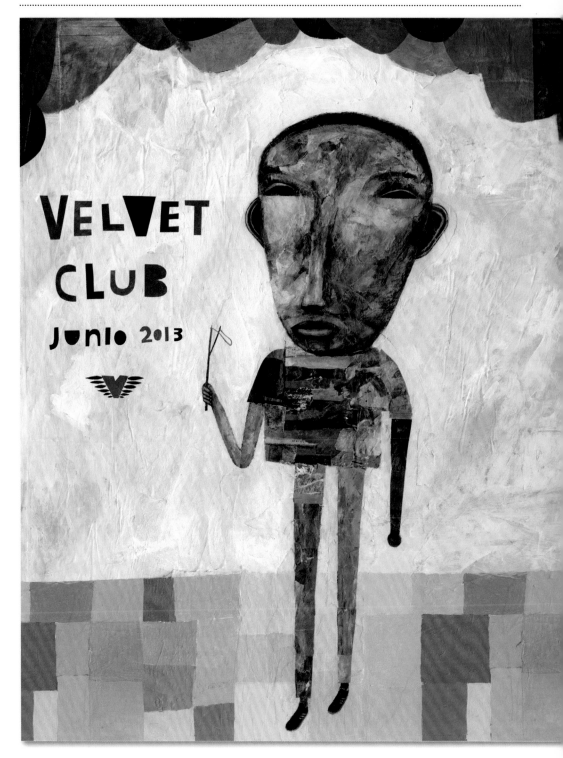

Jordin Isip

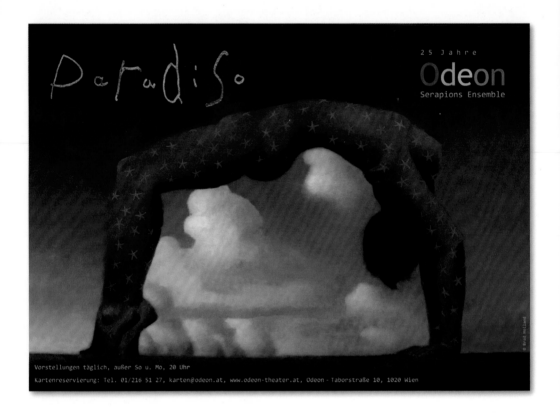

(L) *Brad Holland* (R) *Edel Rodriguez*

Stuart McLachlan

PHILIP GLASS

EINSTEIN ON THE BEACH

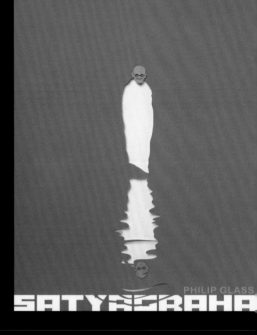

PHILIP GLASS

SATYAGRAHA

LA TRAVIATA

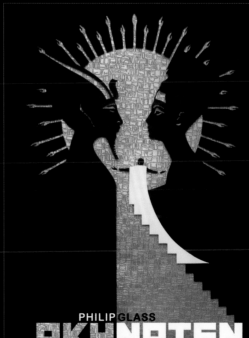

PHILIP GLASS

OKHNATEN

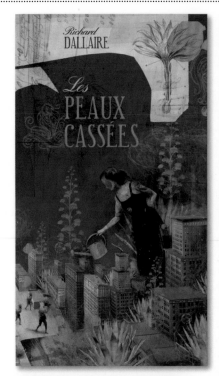

Lars Henkel

Viktor Koen

Brad Holland

Paul Garland

the
amur leopard
total population ~30

the
black rhino
total population 4848

the
cross river gorilla
total population ~300

Nigel Buchanan

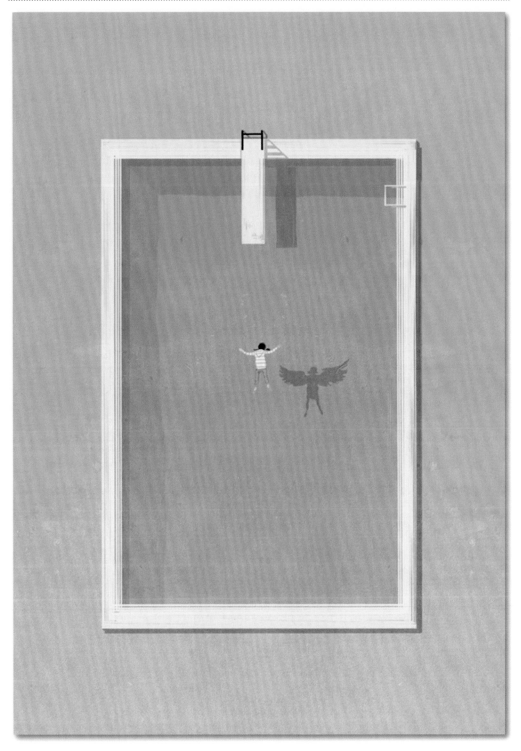

Alessandro Gottardo

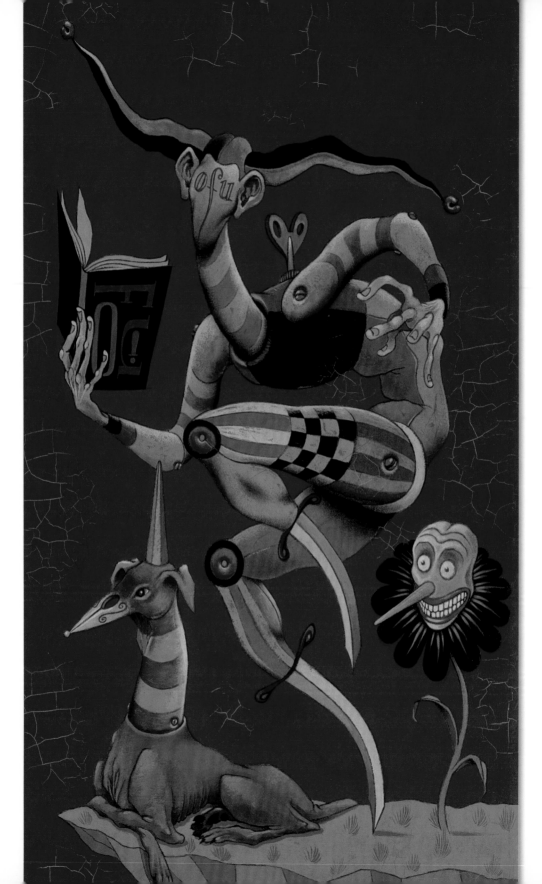

(L) *Pol Turgeon* (R) *Alex Nabaum*

René Milot

Codex Gastropoda

Voluta Musica

A Divination Of Snails

The Burdens Of Knowledge

The Water Daughter's Dream

Gonçalo Viana

Alyssa Winans

René Milot

Douglas Bell

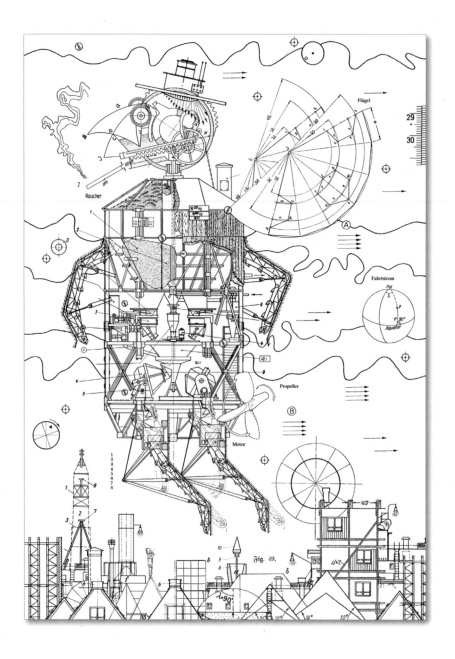

Christian Gralingen

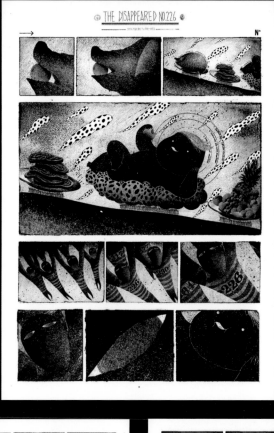

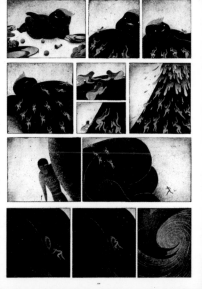

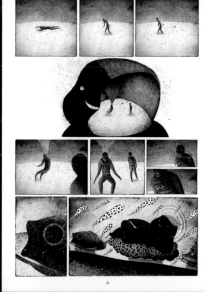

l'ora di lettura

l'abbraccio

la partita al baretto

Douglas Bell

Les Parisiens
the   Parisiens

*une fille marche
dans Montmartre
un jour de neige*

21 Mars 2013

a girl walks
in montmartre
one snowy day
mars 21st 2013

Les Parisiens
the   Parisiens

J'ai vu cette
éblouissante femme
debout à l'arrière-
Plan regardant les
musiciens jouer
Sur le Pont Saint
Louis un jour au
début du printemps

11 Avril 2013

I saw this stunning
woman standing in the
background watching
musicians play on
St Louis Bridge one
day in early spring
April 11th, 2013

Les Parisiens
the   Parisiens

J'ai Rencontré Clara au "Bar Ourq"
le long de Canal de l'Ourq. Selon
elle Sa chevelure particulière vient de
ses origines Bretonnes et Algériennes.
Elle est passionnée par la danse
Bollywoodienne et aimerait partir en Inde
pour apprendre. Elle aime danser d'une
manière générale, Se balader sur
les toits de Paris la nuit, grimper dans
les arbres (sa préférés les Chênes
et les Mimosas), sur les rochers et
marche pieds nus sur le goudron chaud.

27 Juillet 2013

I met Clara at Bar Ourq along
Canal l'Ourq. She says her hair is
from her Breton and Algerian
origins. She loves Bollywood dance
and wants to go to India to study.
She loves to climb trees (oak and
mimosa are her favorites) and rocks,
walk on the rooftops of Paris at night,
and walk barefoot on the hot pavement.

Sug 27, 2013

Les Parisiens
the   Parisiens

J'ai rencontre Vivien et Brian
dans le métro ligne 7, Station
Crimée. Vivien se bat tout
les jours pour réussir sa
passion, la danse. Il est
amoureux de l'être humain
et aime rencontre les gens,
apprendre à les Connaître,
Partager leurs passions,
leurs cultures.

27 Mars 2013

I met Vivien and Brian on the
line 7 Metro at Crimée station.
Vivien fights everyday for his passion,
dance. He loves humanity and loves
meeting people and learning about
them, their passion, and culture.

March 27, 2013

Les Parisiens
the   Parisiens

J'ai rencontre Solenne
autour de Paris à plusieurs
fois. Elle est le Sommelier
à le 6 Paul Bert dans le
11 éme arrondissement.
Elle est
Franco-Vietnamienne
et aimerait visiter
le Vietnam.

3 Septembre 2013

I met Solenne several times
around Paris. She is the
Sommelier at 6 Paul Bert in
the 11th arrondissement. She
is French-Vietnamese and
wants to visit Vietnam.

September 3, 2013

Marion Arbona

(L) *Zara Picken* (R) DISTINGUISHED MERIT *Miguel Montaner*

(L) *Lasse Skarbovik* (R) *Mirko Cresta*

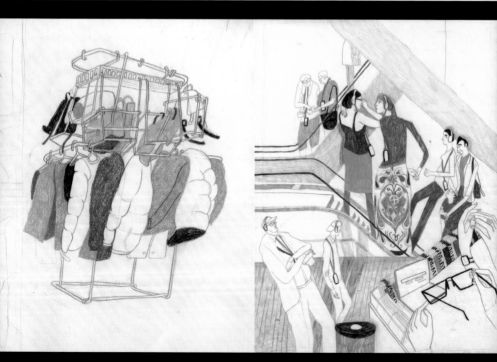

Keren Katz

Livia Cives

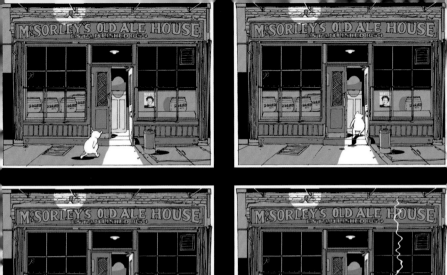

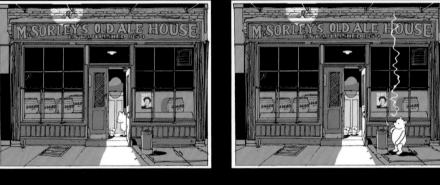

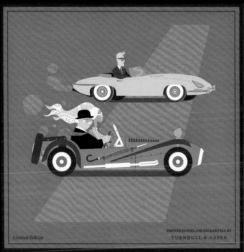

Sarah Jacoby

Andrew J. Nilsen

BRONZE *Jamie Wignall*

Michael Waraksa

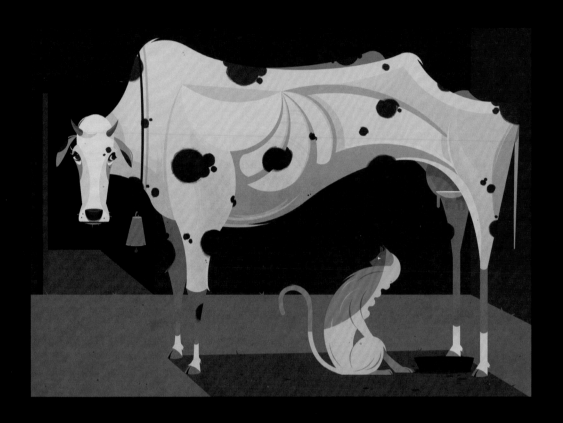

Nicholas Little

Michael Glenwood

Frank Hoppmann

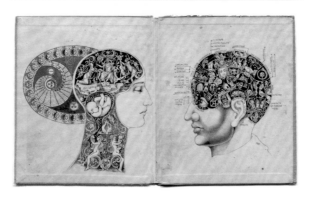

(L) *Sveta Dorosheva* (R) *Bill Mayer*

(L) *Jai Kamat* (R) *Michael Glenwood*

Trudi Esberger

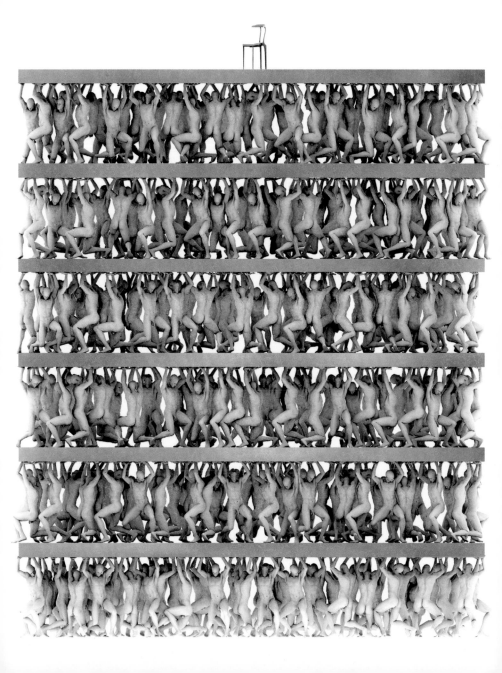

Hanna Barczyk

Sébastien Thibault

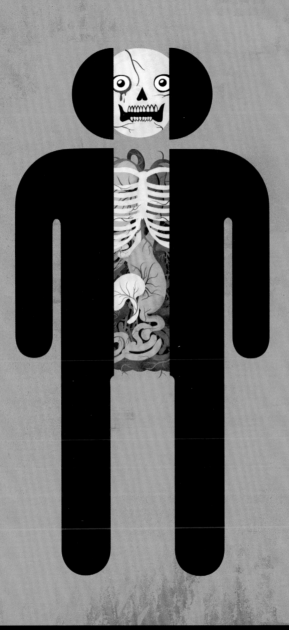

Olivier St-Laurent

Ella Cohen

Miguel Montaner

Michael Waraksa

BRONZE *Seo Kim*

Logan Wagoner

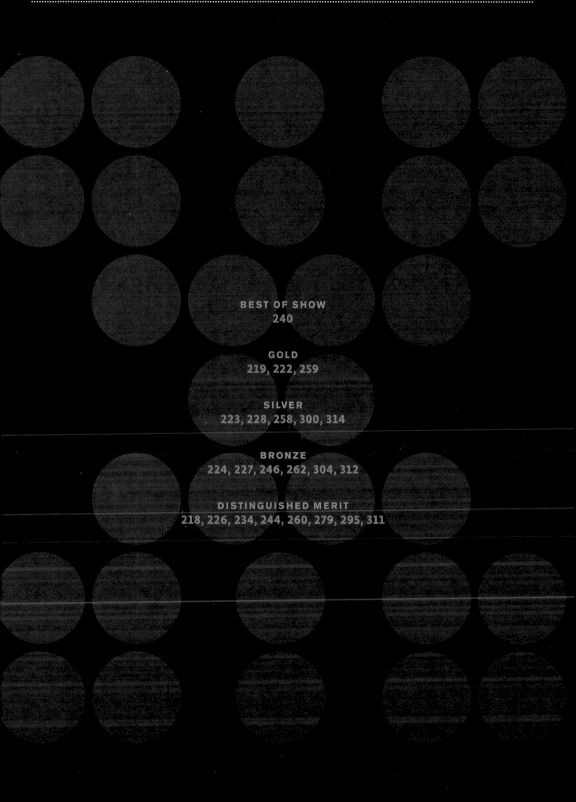

BEST OF SHOW
240

GOLD
219, 222, 259

SILVER
223, 228, 258, 300, 314

BRONZE
224, 227, 246, 262, 304, 312

DISTINGUISHED MERIT
218, 226, 234, 244, 260, 279, 295, 311

AIRBORNE An Anthology of The Real
by Quail Bell Magazine

THE NEST An Anthology of The Unreal
by Quail Bell Magazine

(T,B) **DISTINGUISHED MERIT** *Kristen Rebelo* (R) **GOLD** *Yue Wang*

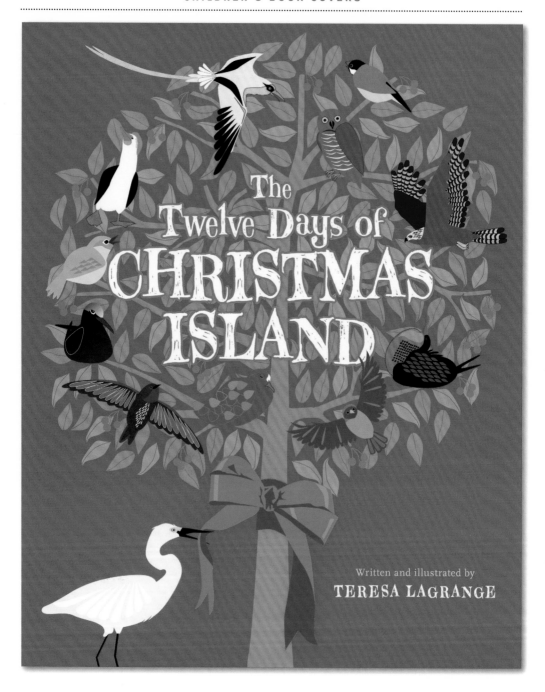

The Twelve Days of CHRISTMAS ISLAND

Written and illustrated by
TERESA LAGRANGE

(L) *Teresa Lagrange* (R) *David Dean*

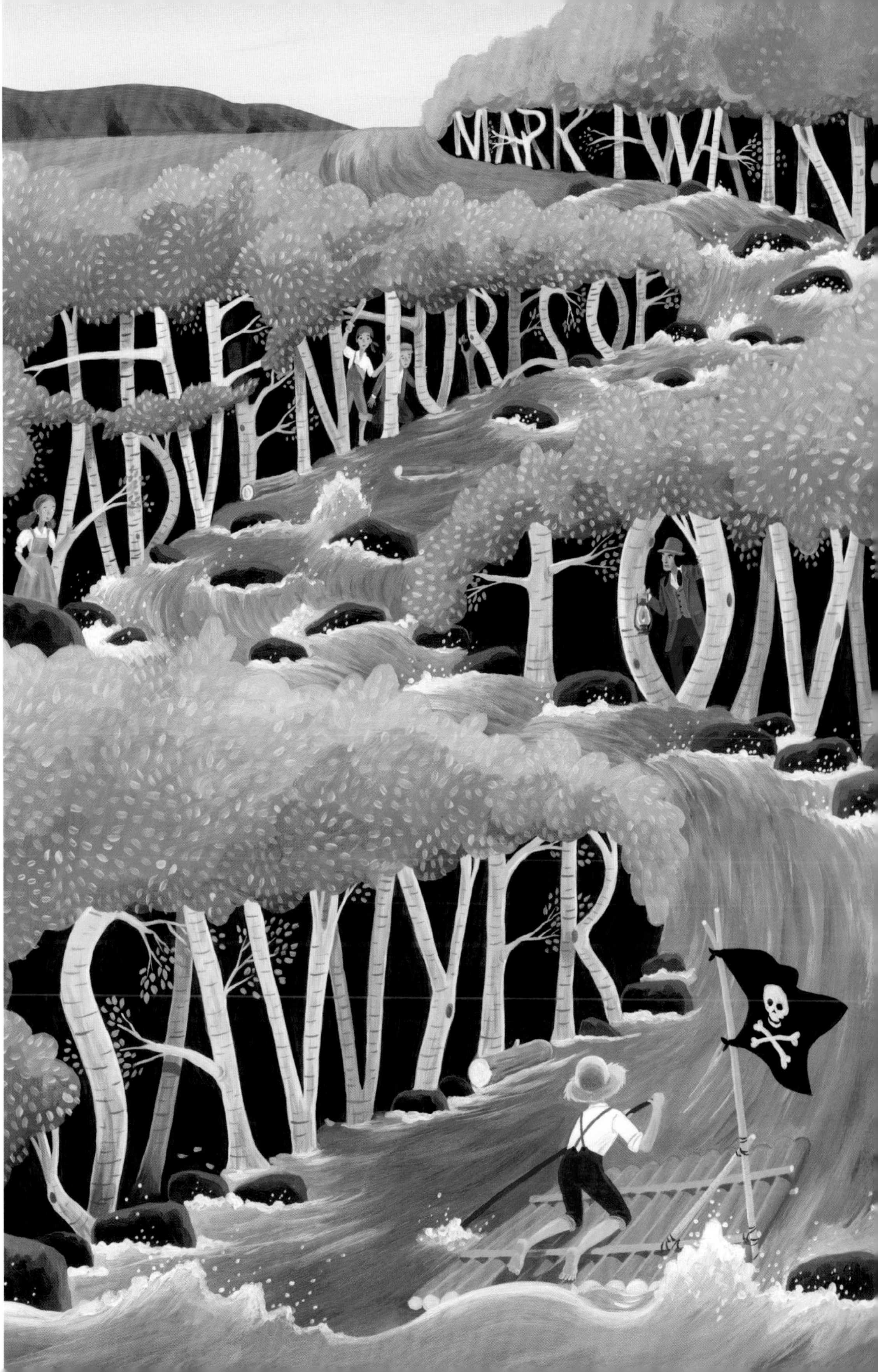
MARK TWAIN
THE ADVENTURES OF
TOM
SAWYER

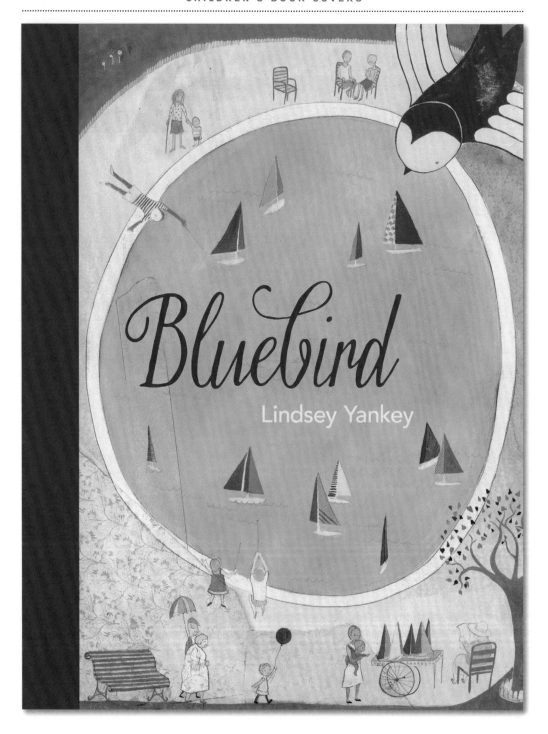

GOLD *Lindsey Yankey*

SILVER *André Letria*

BRONZE *Gwen Keraval*

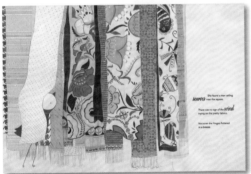

Lindsey Yankey

DISTINGUISHED MERIT *John Parra*

Valentina Mendicino

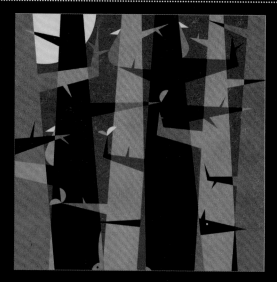

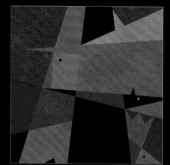

Sara Cunha

Gianni
Biondillo

Il mio
amico Asdrubale

OLTRINDA

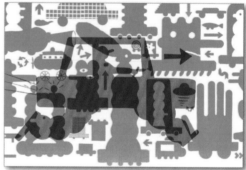

André da Loba

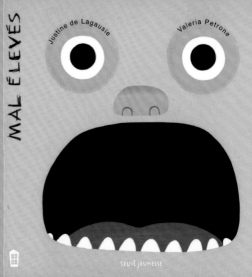

Et c'est nous qu'on traite de mal élevés ?

OKIDOKID a mis sa créativité
au service de ce livre.
© Éditions du Seuil, 2014
25, bd Romain Rolland,
75014 Paris - Dépôt légal : juin 2014
ISBN : 979-10-235-0225-1
Tirage n°1 - Loi 49-956 du 16 juillet 1949
sur les publications destinées à la jeunesse
Imprimé en Chine - www.seuil.com

9,90€

MAL ÉLEVÉS

Justine de Lagausie

Valeria Petrone

seuil jeunesse

9 791023 502251

JE SUIS
LE BABOUIN.

JE SUIS
LE CHIMPANZÉ.

JE SUIS
LE CROCODILE.

JE SUIS
LA GRENOUILLE.

DISTINGUISHED MERIT *Marta Monteiro*

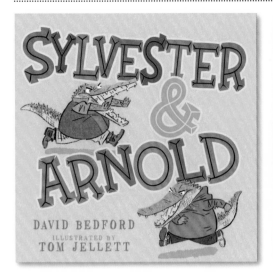

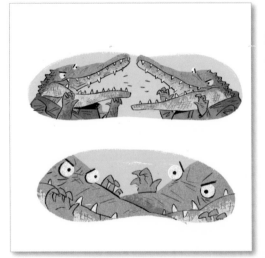

Tom Jellett

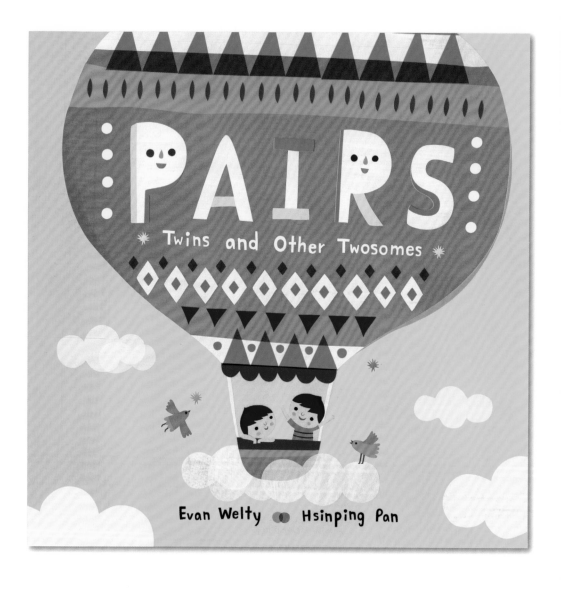

Hsinping Pan

JUNKYARD

Mike Austin

A yard full of junk!
Piles of junk!
Junk as far as the eye can see—
not even room for one little tree.

They chomp many mounds of shopping carts,
picture frames and bicycles,
broken chairs, blue birds
and squeaking furry tricycles.

They slurp truckloads of stinky fish oil,
barrels of sticky paste,
a swimming pool of gooey goo,
and tubs of toxic waste!

BURP!
OIL

They pile dirt high
to make mountains for hiking
and a long winding trail
for running and biking.

(L) *Mike Austin* (R) *Shahar Kober*

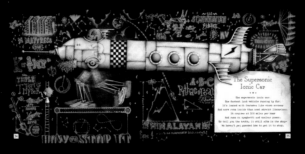

BEST OF SHOW *Jeremy Holmes*

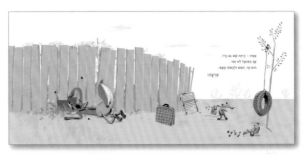

Omer Hoffmann

Giulia Sagramola

DISTINGUISHED MERIT *Natalie Pudalov*

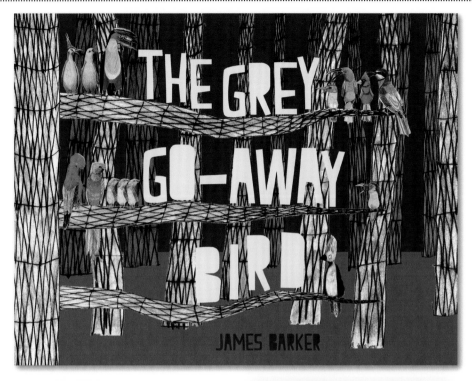

James Barker

(L) **BRONZE** *Scott Murphy* (R) *Christina Hess*

(L) *Annie Won* (R) *Annie Won*

The Button Book

Written by Ricky Friesem

Illustrated by Doron Sohari

Doron Sohari Shemesh

Eiichiro Kato

Alistar

A house glowed warmly in the darkness. If he could just get there, he'd be safe.

SNATCH!
GRAB!
SNAG!

A swarm of ghostly ghouls sprang upon him. Shapeless tentacles clutched at him. Twisting and turning, he spun free.

Scuffy peeked around the corner. His abandoned post beckoned from the cornfield. "Who would protect the crop? If I give up, I'll never be a good scarecrow." He looked at the dancing ghosts. They had buttons and pockets and sleeves. Beyond the clothes flapping in the breeze, he saw the flickering orange monsters! They're just Jack-o-Lanterns. I don't have to be afraid." A smile crossed Scuffy's face. "Well, if I am not scary enough, I'll just make something that is!" Scuffy gathered his supplies and went to work.

"Let go! Let me go!" the bird bawled. Scuffy stared deep into his beady eyes. Securing the snare, Scuffy offered the crow a deal. "You and your boys leave my cornfield alone from now until forever, and I'll let you go."

"I promise! I promise!" croaked the crow.

At dawn Scuffy tucked a black feather in his hat and surveyed his field of plump corn. The sky was clear and clean, not a crow to be seen. He knew it would stay that way because, after all, Scuffy was a scarecrow.

Greg Newbold

Daniel Bueno

Marion Arbona

(L) SILVER *André Letria* (R) GOLD *Marion Arbona*

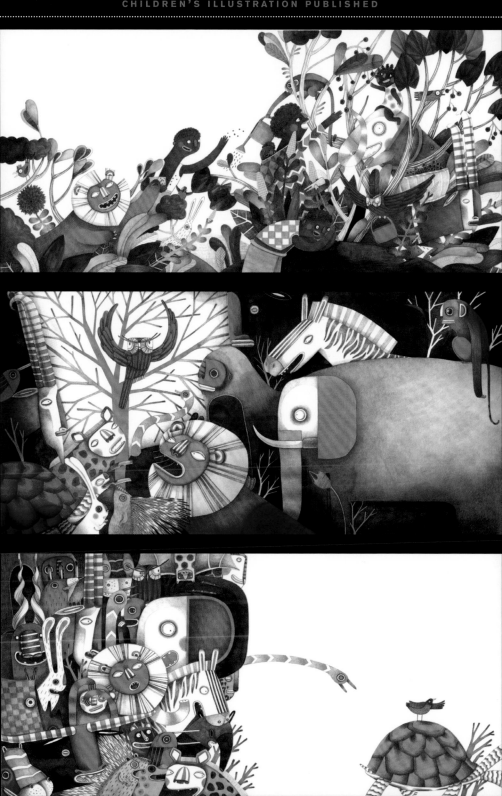

Sleep Like a Rabbit

Sleep like a rabbit, sleep like a bear.
Sleep like the old cat under the chair.
Sleep like a rabbit, sleep like a bear.
Sleep like the old cat under the chair.

Tuck in your paws and lower your head.
Close your blinking eyes so red.
Take a deep breath on your rabbit bed
And now lie down.

Sleep like a polar bear asleep in the sea,
Flat on his back afloat in the sea,
Up on the waves like a boat in the sea,
Snoozing away like a bear on the sea.

Sleep like a rabbit, sleep like a bear.
Sleep like the old cat under the chair.
Sleep like a rabbit, sleep like a bear.
Sleep like the old cat under the chair.

Why so sleepy little mole,
Curled and tightly sleeping?
There is no noise beneath the ground
And no worms sing.

Little squirrel up in a tree,
Resting there so sleepily,
Fluffy tail about your head
In your little wind-rocked bed.
Curl up there so sleepy.

Sleep like a rabbit, sleep like a bear.
Sleep like the old cat under the chair.
Sleep like a rabbit, sleep like a bear.
Sleep like the old cat under the chair.

DISTINGUISHED MERIT *Isabel Roxas*

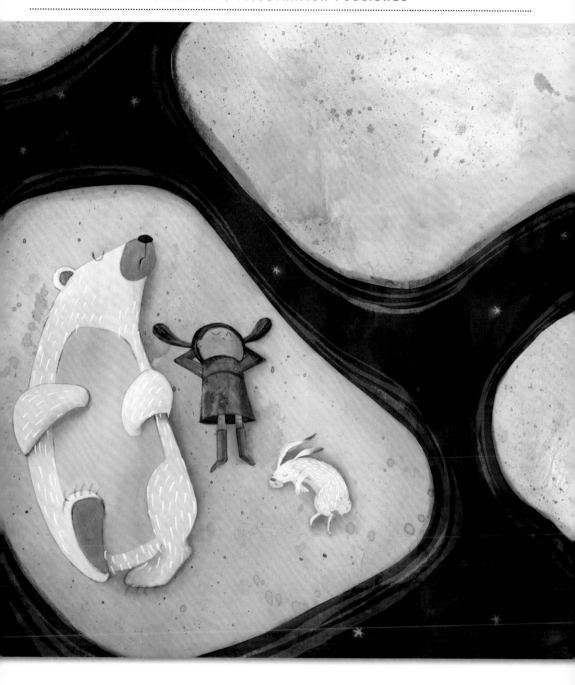

Hideko Yasu

(T) *Dianna Xu* (B) *Sari Cohen*

Ziyue Chen

hello?

Brian Won

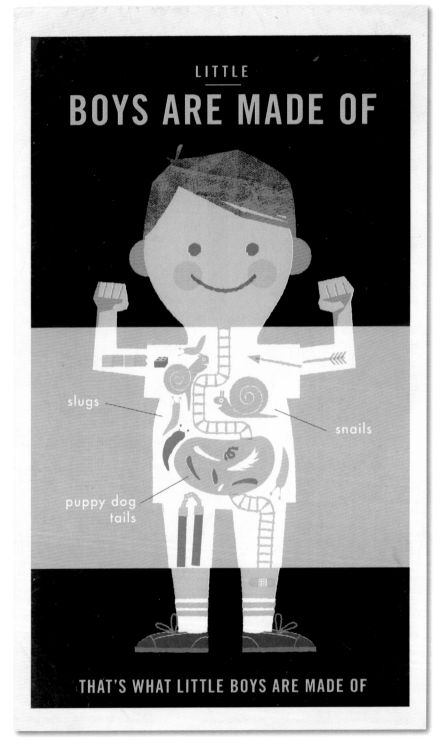

Brian Won

Julien Chung

Ziyue Chen

Jennifer L. Meyer

Coen Hamelink

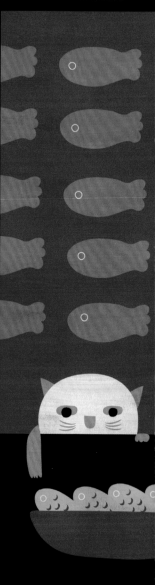

Julia Griffin

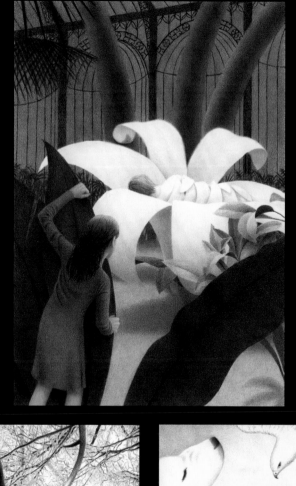

Alexander Vidal

(L) *Jamil Dar* (R) *Estrella Vega*

Hans Baltzer
Christa Holtei

Die Wiese

Ein Zoom-Bilderbuch

BELTZ
&Gelberg

Feldhase

- ► lebt tagsüber in Erdmulden
- ► frisst Pflanzen, Knollen, Wurzeln, Rinde
- ► läuft bei Gefahr 70 Stundenkilometer und schlägt Haken
- ► ist 42–68 cm groß; Ohren 8–12 cm

Beagle

- ► seit über 1000 Jahren Meute-/Jagdhund
- ► lebt erst seit 100 Jahren auch in Häusern
- ► hat er eine Jagdspur aufgenommen, ist er kaum zurückzurufen
- ► ist 33–40 cm hoch

Angela Keoghan

Dornröschen

Rotkäppchen

Die vier kunstreichen Brüder

Rumpelstilzchen

Frau Holle

Julien Chung

Robert Neubecker

(L) *Sophia Choi* (R) *Sara Cunha*

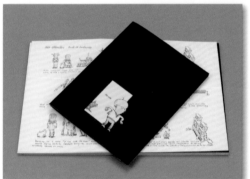

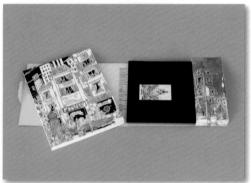

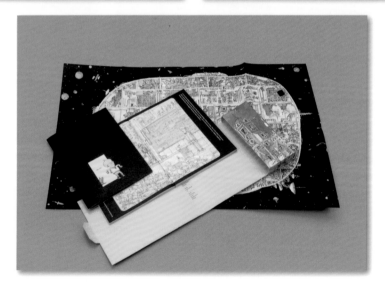

SILVER *Mattias Adolfsson*

Danae Diaz

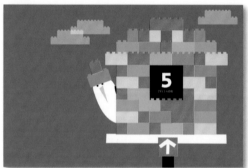

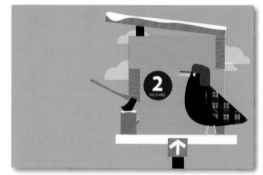

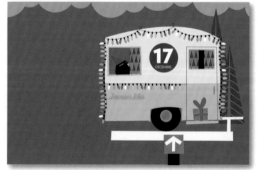

Julien Chung

BRONZE *Marion Arbona*

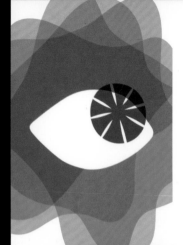

Ecos de Verano

El mundo habla de hombres
que beseñaron su linaje,
y que en medio de su viaje,
evocaron un ciclón.

Y cual joven alquimista,
fuera plebeyo o realeza,
aprendieron: la destreza
de hablar con el corazón
y así cantar la canción
que el tiempo una vez cantó.

De ti sólo leyendas oí
y así yo te conocí,
pues cuando te conocí
ya habías cerrado el baúl
que contenía tu cuento,
y de ti mi risa mi llanto,
tú cielo ni carmesí,
tan sólo ascratos ví
en aquellos ojos lejanos.

Y en uno de aquellos viajes,
ataste tu vista al cielo,
y colgado de un lucero
te vestiste de despojo,
y pusiste tu pie en la vía
que guía a la lejanía
donde de noche y de día
siempre se hallaban tus ojos.

Eco de Otoño...

Somos uno ante la vida,
somos uno sólo que tocós,
y ahora, ante los luchiros,
también somos uno.

La Máquina del Tiempo

Hoy un heraldo sin rumo que detraga en un espacio sin limes
hacia las estrellas has detralla de luz de los reales proviene.

Es un eco intangible, la inowhistoriue de una postura,
aesul a indomia etilla, una immortal sueta
llena la tosta de un sueños, el mindeo del mensaje
planeado en el testamento del sucesso.

Vienftros las huellas, circutrira en papel
solentras a la ves demas inciatraiste de nuevo,
aunque no eses el mismo, y concelar tu memoria
incitaroris verdadera y etorna, una y otra vez.

Alma informable

Que tu espíritu cabalgue la dimensión del tiempo
con la anchura de la luz, y la sabiduría del agua,
el lenguaje del timbar, la memoria de la tierra,
y la voz del viento.

Y más que todo nuevo,
nunca olvides el corazón de la vida,
ni que hará libre tomar tu corazón.

Awichalowan

Un lazo carmín
fue hilo de esposanza
que fortaleció la alianza
de un plebeyo y una flor,
y que abolió aquel temor que acecha
a los que por naturaleza
siguen su fuego interior.

La enseñante a aquel plebeyo,
a huir al remordimiento
y abolió su sentimiento
que cegaba su corazón.

Protegiste la vocación
de aquel plebeyo silence
y fuiste la confidente
de los secretos que habló,
incluyendo uno del fuego
y el preludio del ciclón.

Y un plebeyo debe todo
y torne nada,
y hasta a veces,
los alianzos lo rechazan.

Más después del precipicio hubo alas
que hicieron que aquella ancla volara.
Y un plebeyo se hizo arcángel
para luchar por los que amaba,
y regar con fina luz la colorida flor
que en tinieblas habitaba.

Una flor, un gran cariño,
una huella indeleble...

Isabel Roxas

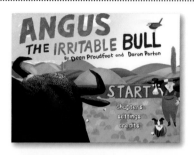

Daron Parton

Il Quaderno quadrone
di
Loredana Lipperini
con illustrazioni di
Paolo d'Altan
Introduzione di
Lidia Ravera

PUPA

RS Rrose Sélavy

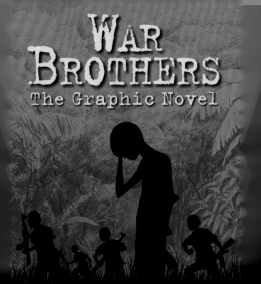

WAR BROTHERS
The Graphic Novel

SHARON E. McKAY • DANIEL LAFRANCE

DISTINGUISHED MERIT *Katie Kath*

O. Henry & Sonja Danowski

THE GIFT OF
THE MAGI

BRONZE *Sonja Danowski*

RÜCKKEHR IN DIE NACHT

CLEMENS MEYER

Illustriert von PHILLIP JANTA

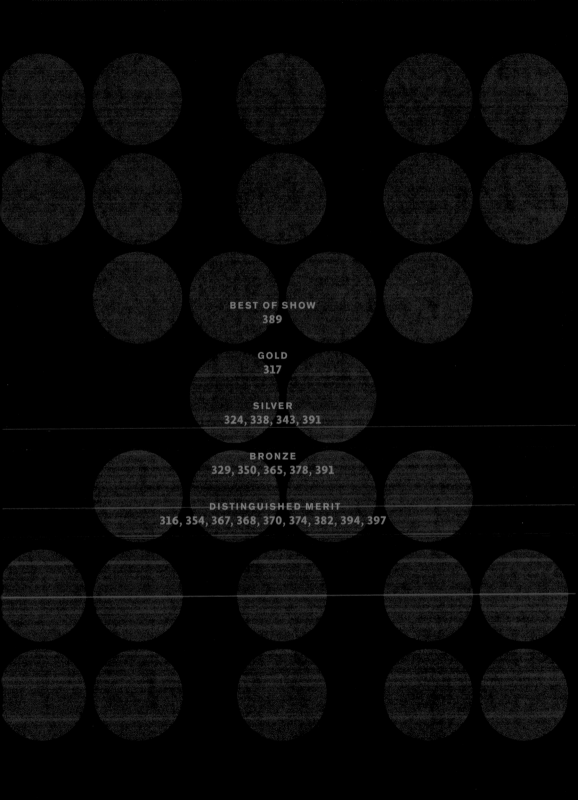

BEST OF SHOW
389

GOLD
317

SILVER
324, 338, 343, 391

BRONZE
329, 350, 365, 378, 391

DISTINGUISHED MERIT
316, 354, 367, 368, 370, 374, 382, 394, 397

(L) DISTINGUISHED MERIT *German Herrera* (M) *Chen Winner*
(R) GOLD *Janice Ahn, A.J. Bae, Zach Eastburg, Yoon Sun Lee*

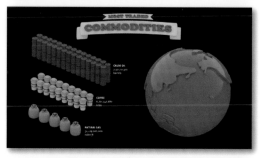

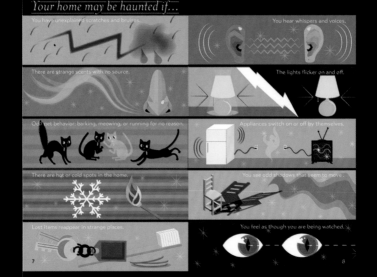

You have unexplained scratches and bruises.

You hear whispers and voices.

There are strange scents with no source.

The lights flicker on and off.

Odd pet behavior: barking, meowing, or running for no reason.

Appliances switch on or off by themselves.

There are hot or cold spots in the home.

You see odd shadows that seem to move.

Lost items reappear in strange places.

You feel as though you are being watched.

7

8

Even "tough guys" may feel intense, physical fear symptoms in the presence of a paranormal entity. They...

Witching hours

The best time to look for ghosts is between 8 am and 3 am.

However, most museums say:

Paranormal phenomena are strongest between 3 am and 4 am.

Plan accordingly.

The GHOST in the MACHINE

In an ordinary film camera, light exposure causes chemical changes on the surface of the film, resulting in images that may later be developed. Some natural presences are thought to be able to cause these chemical alterations directly, without light.

35

34

…Most ghosts use their electromagnetic sensitivity to imprint directly onto the magnetic heads of analogue tape.

Digital recording devices have one major drawback: they record sound. Some ghosts appear able to make audible sounds, but…

35

36

Meredith Bentley

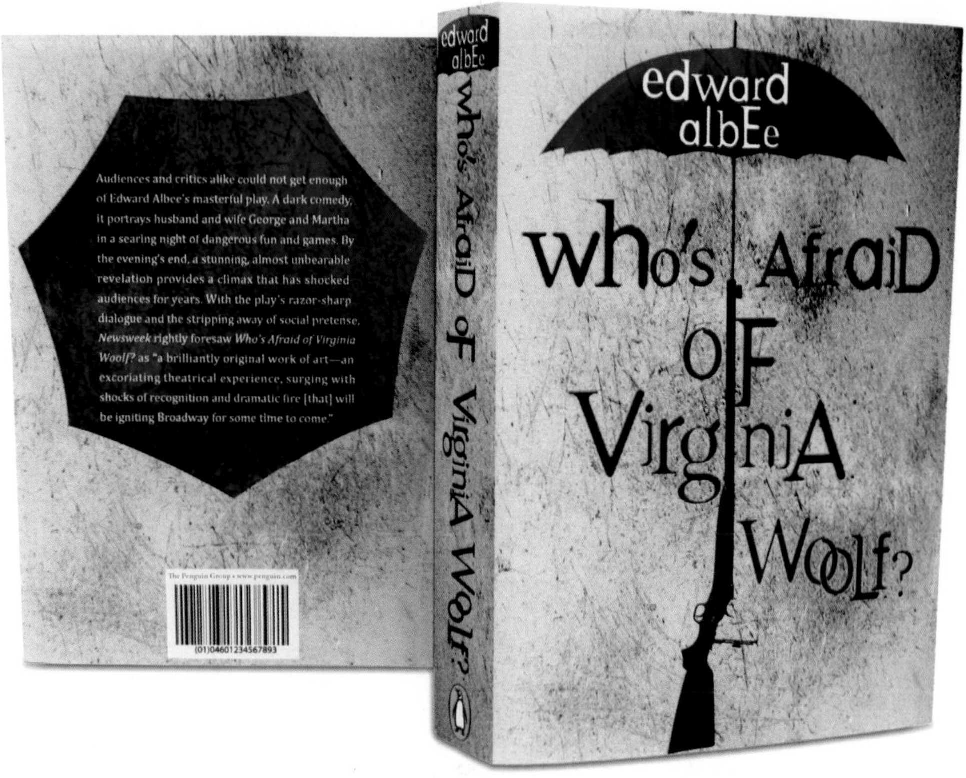
Audiences and critics alike could not get enough of Edward Albee's masterful play. A dark comedy, it portrays husband and wife George and Martha in a searing night of dangerous fun and games. By the evening's end, a stunning, almost unbearable revelation provides a climax that has shocked audiences for years. With the play's razor-sharp dialogue and the stripping away of social pretense, Newsweek rightly foresaw Who's Afraid of Virginia Woolf? as "a brilliantly original work of art—an excoriating theatrical experience, surging with shocks of recognition and dramatic fire [that] will be igniting Broadway for some time to come."
The Penguin Group • www.penguin.com
(01)04601234567893
edward albEe
who's AfraiD of VirginiA WoOlf?
edward albEe
who's AfraiD oF VirginjA WoOLf?

Joshua Marz

(L) *Celia Favorite* (R) *Moonsub Shin*

Luke Marcatili

Tina Furesz

SILVER *Eitan Eloa*

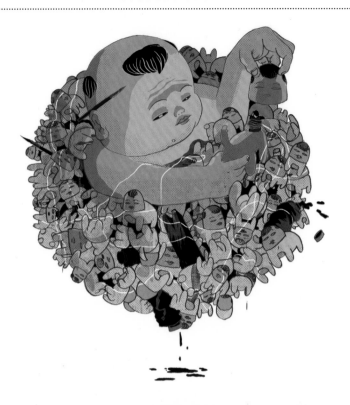

(T) *Jori van der Linde* (B) *Erin McManness*

(T) BRONZE *Seo Kim* (BL) *Brenna Thummler* (BR) *Maria Nguyen*

Han-Yuan Yu

(T) *Yohey Horishita* (B) *Jing Li*

Kristen Davis

(T) *Naomi Butterfield* (B) *Elyse Salazar*

Cristian Fowlie

SILVER *Cyndi Waldron*

(T) *Ai Zhang* (BL) *Dorian Lafferre* (BR) *Jordan Walsh*

Greg Wright

Grant Kratzer

(L) *Yohey Horishita* (R) SILVER *Lisk Feng*

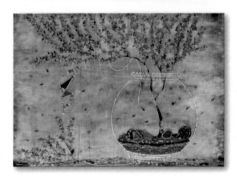

M. Poppit

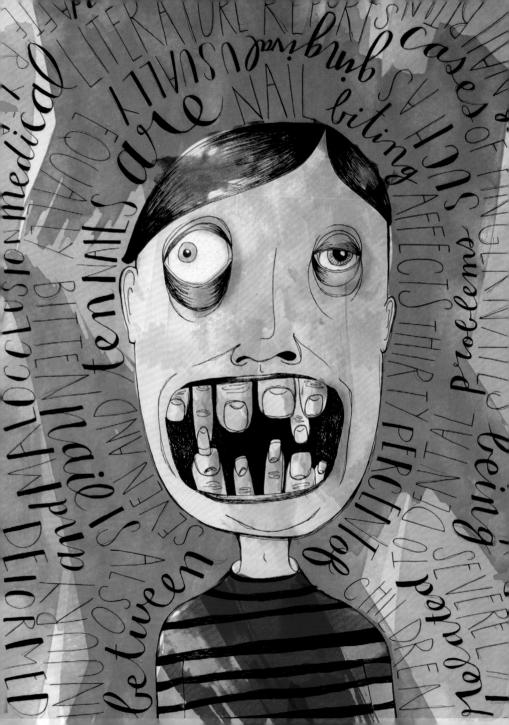

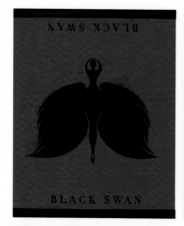

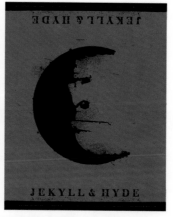

Max Amato

Tsung-Yun Wan

BRONZE *Leonard Peng*

Sue Jean Ko

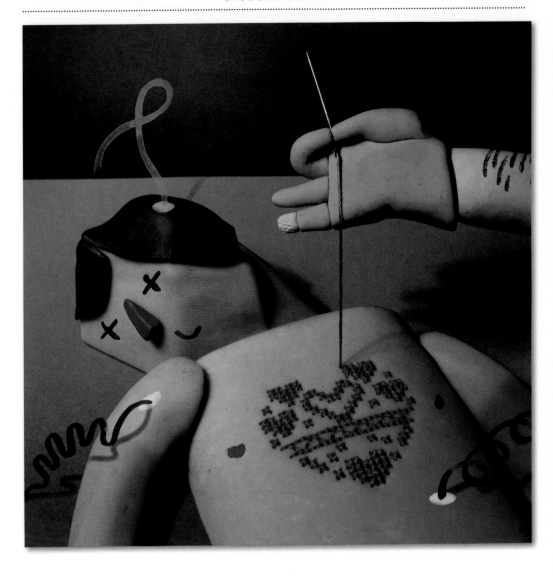

DISTINGUISHED MERIT *Hudson Christie*

Xiaohua Yang

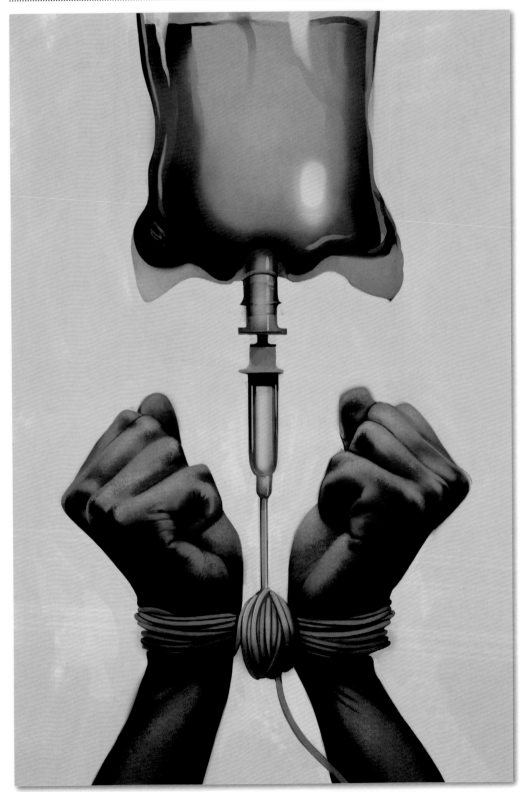

Hudson Christie

Lisa Oh

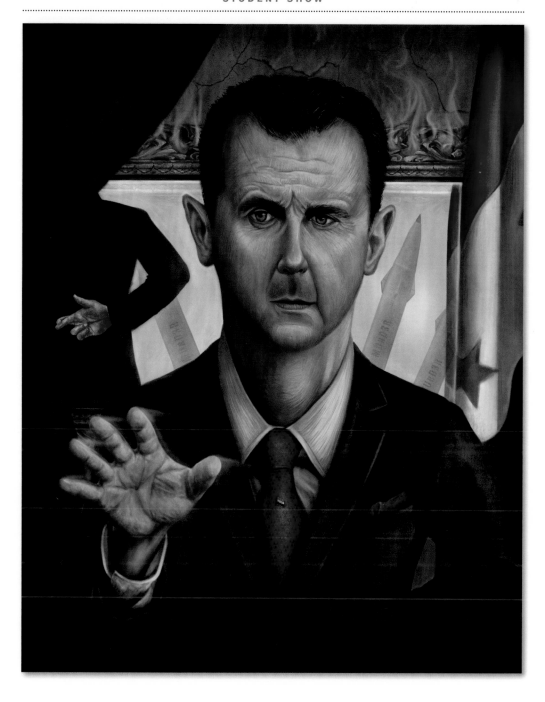

Tylor Heagy

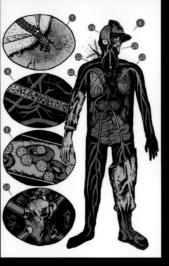

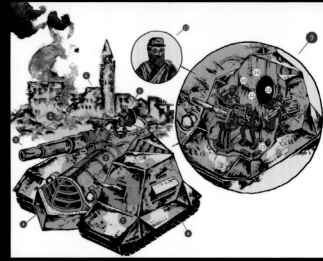

(L) *Tom Wiklund* (T) *Tylor Heagy* (B) BRONZE *Sophie Geneva Page*

Evan Worsham

(L) **DISTINGUISHED MERIT** *Riikka Laakso* (R) *Kristin Chae*

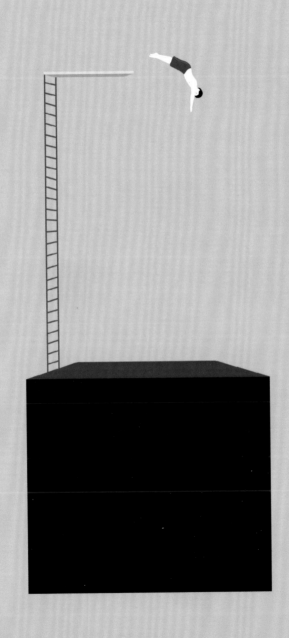

Shane Lewis

Chris Chai

DISTINGUISHED MERIT *Janet Croog*

André Wee

Neta Hagiladi-Finkelstein

Nancy Liang

BRONZE *Marilyn Foehrenbach*

(T) *Giulio Bonasera* (B) *Xiaohua Yang*

ELLE REGARDE SES AMIES TOMBER, CRAINTIVE
VOLER, VIREVOLTER, VIVRE ET MOURIR
LA FEUILLE ATTEND LA CHUTE DANS LA BRISE VIVE
SI RAPIDE POUR TANT DE SOUVENIRS

PATIEMMENT LE GEL RONGE LES COURANTS
PENDANT QUE LE SOLEIL AGITE SON PINCEAU
LES OISEAUX SE CACHENT POUR QUELQUE TEMPS
NATURE S'ENDORT ET SE RÉVEILLE EN SURSAUT

LES FOLIES DE L'ÉTÉ SONT PASSÉES
L'HORIZON PROGRESSIVEMENT GRISONNE
BIENTÔT TOUS RÉUNIS DEVANT LA CHEMINÉE
MAIS PEUT-ÊTRE L'AIMONS- NOUS CET AUTOMNE

JOANNA MÜLLER

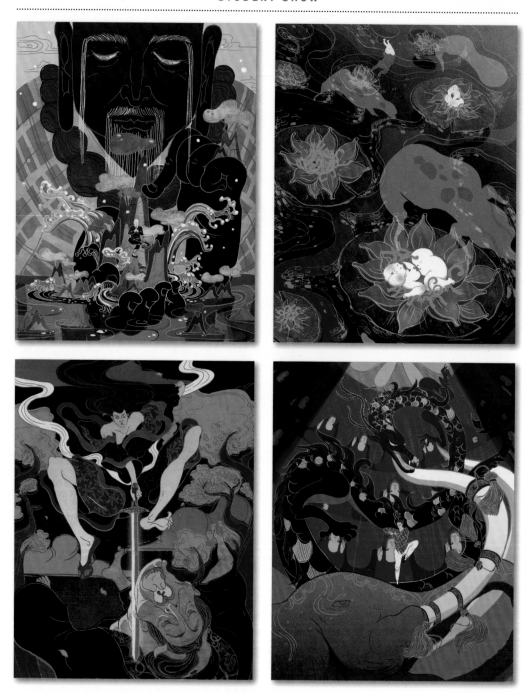

(L) DISTINGUISHED MERIT *Yufei Zhao* (R) *Brenna Thummler*

Amanda Konishi

Ryan Cho

Molly Mendoza

Cameron Cottrill

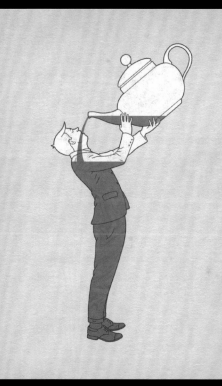

Amanda Konishi

DISTINGUISHED MERIT *Ksenia Kozhevnikova*

Skye Bolluyt

(L) *Pedro Amato* (R) DISTINGUISHED MERIT *Han-Yuan Yu*

Seonhee Lim

Ksenia Kozhevnikova

6x9-INCHES
292-PAGES
ISBN 978-0-9826346-46

{*ILLUSTRATION by BILL MAYER*

THE 2015 3X3 ILLUSTRATION DIRECTORY

WE WANT YOU TO HAVE A COPY OF OUR NEW 3X3 ILLUSTRATION DIRECTORY. AVAILABLE ONLINE OR AS AN APP OR IN PRINT.

UNLIKE OTHER DIRECTORIES OURS IS CURATED, THE IMAGES ARE BROKEN INTO SPECIFIC CATEGORIES AND THE SIZE IS PORTABLE.

YOU'LL DISCOVER 220 ILLUSTRATORS FROM ALL ACROSS THE GLOBE WHO HAVE MET OUR HIGH STANDARDS.

CHECK OUT OUR WEBSITE, GET THE LINK TO THE FREE IOS APP AND
REQUEST A FREE COPY OF THE DIRECTORY*

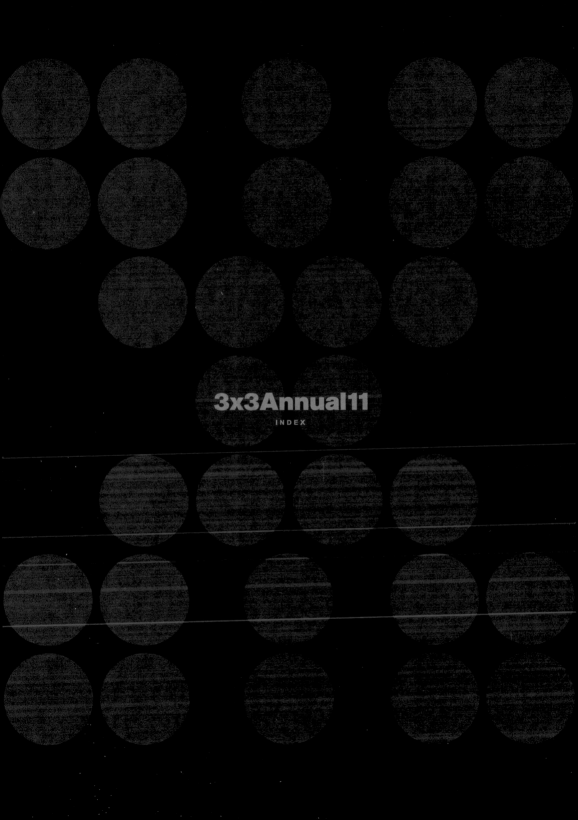

3x3Annual11
INDEX

INDEX

INDEX